Building a Better Bridge

Building a Better Bridge

Muslims, Christians, and the Common Good

A record of the fourth Building Bridges seminar
held in Sarajevo, Bosnia-Herzegovina, May 15–18, 2005

Michael Ipgrave, Editor

Georgetown University Press ✌ Washington, DC

Georgetown University Press, Washington, D.C. www.press.georgetown.edu
© 2008 by Georgetown University Press. All rights reserved. No part of this
book may be reproduced or utilized in any form or by any means, electronic or
mechanical, including photocopying and recording, or by any information stor-
age and retrieval system, without permission in writing from the publisher.

Library of Congress Cataloging-in-Publication Data

Building a better bridge : Muslims, Christians and the common good : a
record of the fourth "Building bridges" seminar held in Sarajevo,
Bosnia-Herzegovina, May 15–18, 2005 / Michael Ipgrave, editor.
       p.   cm.
   Includes bibliographical references and index.
   ISBN-13: 978-1-58901-221-9 (alk. paper)
   1. Islam—Relations—Christianity—Congresses.   2. Christianity and
other religions—Islam—Congresses.   I. Ipgrave, Michael.
BP172.B83   2008
261.2'7—dc22

                          2008005432

⊗ This book is printed on acid-free paper meeting the requirements of the
American National Standard for Permanence in Paper for Printed Library
Materials.

15 14 13 12 11 10 09 08   9 8 7 6 5 4 3 2
First printing

Printed in the United States of America

Text in Michael Nazir-Ali's essay is reprinted with the kind permission of
Continuum.

Portions of Ellen Davis's essay are reprinted with permission of Cambridge
University Press.

Contents

Participants   vii

About the Seminar   ix

Introduction

    Muslims, Christians, and the Common Good
    Michael Ipgrave   1

Chapter 1   Believers and Citizens

    "In Broken Images": Faith in the Public Sphere
    Maleiha Malik   7

    Christian Faith and National Belonging
    Michael Nazir-Ali   27

    Faith and National Identity of Catholics in Bosnia-Herzegovina
    Mato Zovkic   35

    The Identity of Christians in Church and in State
    Bogdan Lubardič   41

    Faith and National Identity in Britain
    Zaki Badawi and Michael Ipgrave   49

    Notes   59

Chapter 2   Seeking the Common Good

    Islamic Views of the Collective
    Tariq Ramadan   73

    The Common Good: Catholicism, Pluralism, and Secular Society
    John Langan   81

Bosnian Muslim Scholars on Governance and Justice
Fikret Karcic   93

Muslim and Christian Perspectives on Different Models of
Governance and Justice
Vladimir Ciric   97

Government and Religion in Malaysia
Mohammad Hashim Kamali   103

Different Models of Governance and Justice: A West African
Christian Perspective
John Azumah   115

Notes   126

Chapter 3   Caring Together for the World We Share

Christianity, Islam, and the Challenge of Poverty
Rowan Williams   133

Poverty and the Charism of Ishmael
Timothy J. Winter   141

Speaking to the Heart
Ellen F. Davis   153

Āyatology and Raḥmatology: Islam and the Environment
Aref Ali Nayed   161

Notes   168

Conclusion

Building Bridges in Bosnia-Herzegovina
Michael Ipgrave   175

Index   179

Participants

Seyed Amir Akrami
Lecturer, University of Tehran

John Azumah
Senior research fellow, Akrofi-Christaller Memorial Centre, Ghana

M. A. Zaki Badawi
Principal of The Muslim College, London

Vladimir Ciric
Researcher in Christian–Muslim Relations, Belgrade

Vincent J. Cornell
Director, King Fahd Center for Middle East and Islamic Studies, University of Arkansas

Ellen F. Davis
Professor of Bible and Practical Theology, Duke University, Durham, North Carolina

Lejla Demiri
PhD student in divinity, University of Cambridge

Resid Hafizovic
Professor, faculty of Islamic Studies, Sarajevo

Michael Ipgrave
Archdeacon of Southwark, Church of England

Mohammad Hashim Kamali
Dean of International Institute of Islamic Thought and Civilization, Malaysia

Fikret Karcic
Professor, Faculty of Islamic Theology, University of Sarajevo

Enes Karic
Professor of Qur'anic Studies, Faculty of Islamic Studies, Sarajevo

John Langan
Joseph Cardinal Bernardin Professor of Catholic Social Thought, Georgetown University

Bogdan Lubardič
Faculty of Theology, University of Belgrade

Daniel A. Madigan
Director, Institute for the Study of Religions and Cultures, Pontifical Gregorian University, Rome

Maleiha Malik
Lecturer in law at School of Law, King's College, University of London

Aref Ali Nayed
Visiting fellow, The Centre for Advanced Religious and Theological Studies, Faculty of Divinity, University of Cambridge

Michael Nazir-Ali
Bishop of Rochester, Church of
England

Tariq Ramadan
Professor of Islamic Studies at the
University of Fribourg, Switzerland

Mona Siddiqui
Senior lecturer in Arabic and Islamic
Studies and department head of
Theology and Religious Studies,
Glasgow University, Scotland

Miroslav Volf
Henry B. Wright Professor of Theology,
Yale University Divinity School

Rowan Williams
Archbishop of Canterbury, Church of
England

Timothy J. Winter
Lecturer in Islamic Studies, Faculty of
divinity, University of Cambridge

Frances Young
Edward Cadbury Professor of Theology,
University of Birmingham

Mato Zovkic
Professor of Sarajevo Theological
Seminary

About the Seminar

The fourth annual Building Bridges seminar of Christians and Muslims convened by the Archbishop of Canterbury was held in Sarajevo, Bosnia-Herzegovina, May 15–18, 2005. The seminar was cohosted by Rais al-Ulama Dr. Mustafa Ceric, leader of the Muslim community of Bosnia-Herzegovina; Metropolitan Nikolaj of the Serbian Orthodox Diocese of Dabar-Bosnia; and Cardinal Vinko Puljic, the Roman Catholic Archbishop of Sarajevo. The work of organizing the seminar was carried forward at the Bosnian end by staff of the Faculty of Islamic Studies in the University of Sarajevo. As in other Building Bridges seminars, the program included a mixture of public lectures—held in the Bosniak Institute—and closed sessions, in plenary and in small groups—held in the Catholic Theological Faculty. The seminar concluded with a large public reception at the National Theatre, at which the Archbishop of Canterbury and the three senior Bosnian leaders spoke, together with Lord (Paddy) Ashdown, the High Representative for Bosnia-Herzegovina; that evening also included musical and cultural contributions from local young people.

The overall title of the seminar was "Christians, Muslims and the Common Good," and this wide-ranging theme was explored for three days by looking at three successive topics: "Believers and Citizens: Faith and National Identity in Christian and Muslim Perspective," "Seeking the Common Good: Governance and Justice in Christian and Muslim Perspective," and "Caring Together for the World We Share." This volume presents the texts of the public lectures that addressed each of these topics, together with regional presentations on issues of citizenship, religious believing and belonging, and the relationship between government and religion—both from the immediate situation of Bosnia-Herzegovina and from three contexts farther afield: Britain, Malaysia, and West Africa. Unlike in earlier and later Building Bridges seminars, the joint reading of texts did not provide a focus for the program of small group meetings in Sarajevo, and no attempt has been made here to capture the very wide-ranging discussions held in the groups, stimulating as these generally were.

I would like to express my deep appreciation of the work of Ahmet Alibasic, of the Faculty of Islamic Studies in the University of Sarajevo, who not only coordinated practical arrangements for the seminar but also provided audio recordings of the public lectures, which have been invaluable in reconstructing the contributions of Professor Ramadan and Nayed, presented later; of David Marshall, whose meticulous scholarship and sympathetic wisdom have given constant and always reliable guidance to me; and of Richard Brown of Georgetown University Press, whose patient persistence has finally brought this volume to publication.

Introduction

Muslims, Christians, and the Common Good

This volume presents a record of the fourth in the Building Bridges series of international Christian–Muslim seminars, held in Sarajevo, Bosnia-Herzegovina, May 15–18, 2005.[1] Convened by the Archbishop of Canterbury and jointly hosted by Dr. Mustafa Ceric; Rais al-Ulama of the Muslim community of Bosnia-Herzegovina; Metropolitan Nikolaj of the Serbian Orthodox Diocese of Dabar-Bosnia; and Cardinal Vilko Puljic, the Roman Catholic Archbishop of Sarajevo, the theme of the seminar was "Muslims, Christians, and the Common Good." The participants, who met for three days of public lectures and private conversations, had brought home to them the particular poignancy and relevance of this global theme in the Bosnian context. Ten years previously, Serbian Orthodox, Croatian Catholics, and Bosniac Muslims had all been engaged in a series of bitter conflicts where religious belonging had been implicated with ethnicity and culture in a complex nexus of contested identities. Now, as all communities faced the challenge of building a nation and a civic society, the challenge facing Christians and Muslims was to move on from identity-based politics to ask about the resources each could bring from the riches of their tradition to offer to the common good.[2] Given the continuing scars people bore from the enmities of the past, this was no mean challenge, but contributions from locally based Catholics, Orthodox, and Muslims helped to ground and focus the seminar's discussions of global themes by constantly bringing them back to this one particular context. Four presentations from the former Yugoslavia are included in this volume, along with three case studies from other parts of the world.

The eight public lectures also presented here show Christian and Muslim scholars engaging from the depths and riches of their own traditions with three

I

key questions to be faced in addressing the issue of the common good. First, how do we approach the civic sphere as believers in particular faiths and as citizens of mixed societies; what makes us who we are; and how do our religious and secular allegiances relate to one another? Second, what is it in our religions that motivates us to seek the common good; how do we accommodate our commitment to divinely mandated values with acknowledgment of human disagreement; and how can this be expressed in models of governance and justice? Third, how are we to respond to the current disorder of our world in light of the vision of divine purpose that we have received; what resources do our traditions have to equip us in our economic and ecological crisis; and how can we pass on to our endangered and contested planet the prophetic challenge of peace and justice that our scriptures convey? These are questions whose importance is only exceeded by their immensity and complexity; the record that follows does not, of course, claim to provide definitive answers, but it does include insights and reflections that should be of benefit to Christians, Muslims, and everyone committed to seeking the common good for our societies.

Notes

1. Previous seminars are presented in the following volumes, all edited by Michael Ipgrave and published by Church House Publishing, London: Lambeth (2002) in *The Road Ahead: A Christian-Muslim Dialogue;* Doha (2003) in *Scriptures in Dialogue: Christians and Muslims Studying the Bible and the Qur'ān Together;* and Georgetown (2004) in *Bearing the Word: Prophecy in Biblical and Qur'ānic Perspective.*
2. Paddy Ashdown, the UN's High Representative in Bosnia-Herzegovina, commenting on the tenth anniversary of the Dayton Accords of 1995, observed: "Although we have created institutions, we have not created a civil society" (interview in *The Guardian*, November 2, 2005).

Chapter 1

✧

Believers and Citizens

How do two senses of belonging relate—to a universal religion and to a particular society? How do two senses of allegiance relate—to God and to a state? How do two senses of identity relate—as believers and as citizens? These questions have been posed throughout both Christian and Muslim history, and a variety of answers have been given to them. Context has been a critically important factor in shaping not only the answers but also, prior to that, the very way in which the questions are shaped, as the following essays and presentations demonstrate.

It may be generally true that these tensions have been more sharply felt within Christianity than within Islam; indeed, some interpreters of Islamic thought and some projects for Islamic society have sought to abolish the distinctions of "temporal" and "spiritual" altogether. For Muslims and Christians alike, though, the questions are posed with particular clarity and urgency in societies dominated by a liberal secular attitude that seeks to demarcate civic and religious by equating them with, respectively, public and private. Maleiha Malik's essay challenges the fundamental presuppositions of this way of thinking by radically questioning the availability of genuinely neutral space, whether rooted in secularity or in religion. She insists on continuity between private and public identities and argues that the practice of the virtue of justice should be carried over from the individual to the social field. Applied to her own religious tradition, she shows how this approach will bring Islam and modernity into a mutually critical dialogue likely to prove particularly sharp and stimulating for Muslim minorities in the West.

While Western Muslim communities may find themselves in a comparatively unfamiliar place in terms of Islamic tradition, minority status is in

3

some ways much more deeply embedded in the narrative of the Christian Church, as Michael Nazir-Ali's essay acknowledges. However, he also demonstrates how, from biblical times onward, there has been a constant interplay between "church" and "state," finding expression in a wide range of Christian attitudes to, and a variety of patterns of involvement with, the ruling authorities. He traces in particular developments in post-Reformation Anglicanism, showing how there grows here both recognition of a proper sphere for each and an encouragement of interaction between the two; he refers to this dynamic in the characteristically Anglican language of "creative tension."

Both Malik as a Muslim and Nazir-Ali as a Christian, then, trace a relationship between the two senses of belonging, allegiance and identity, which goes beyond either civic secularism on the one hand or religious totalism on the other hand. It is a relationship that, rightly understood and practiced, places believers who are also citizens at the intersection of a double sense of participation, through which their multilayered identities will be formed by a dialogical and dialectic interaction of faith and citizenship that is always shaped by particular contexts.

Some of the practical working out of this general approach in given situations can then be traced in the following three case studies. Mato Zovkic, speaking as a Catholic priest of Croat ethnic background who is a citizen of Bosnia-Herzegovina, explores the way in which civic, ethnic, and religious senses of belonging are played out in political life, in light of the guidance afforded by contemporary Catholic teaching. Also writing from the perspective of the former Yugoslavia, Bogdan Lubardič as a Serbian Orthodox believer discusses the relationship of Christian identity, as liturgically formed in the church, with citizenship of a particular state and explains the Serbian mediation of these in the historical way of *svetosavlje*, which he interprets as involving both mutual cooperation and simultaneous differentiation between church and state. Both Zovkic and Lubardič write out of a context that has been sharply and tragically contested in recent years. In contrast, Zaki Badawi and Michael Ipgrave address the British situation, which has developed in a much more evolutionary way; yet they acknowledge that even here tensions are apparent. Writing together as Muslim and Christian, they show how both minority and majority communities are struggling to adjust to a new situation that fundamentally interrogates both theological and political senses of identity. They insist that, as Muslims and Christians find themselves facing some of the same issues of believing and belonging in the modern world, it is essential that they should retrieve a sense of the complex histories of their communities which have formed the present through the past and which will help to shape the future.

"In Broken Images"

Faith in the Public Sphere

✑

Maleiha Malik

Why, when this span of life might be fleeted away . . .
Oh, why have to be human, and, shunning Destiny, long for Destiny? . . .
Not out of curiosity, not just to practice the heart, . . .
But because being here is much, and because all this
That's here, so fleeting, seems to require us and strangely concerns us.
Us the most fleeting of all. Just once, everything, only for once. Once and no more.

But into the other relation,
What, alas! Do we carry across? Not the beholding we've here
Slowly acquired, and no here occurrence. Not one.
Sufferings, then. Above all, the hardness of life,
The long experience of love; in fact,
Pure untellable things . . .

Here is the time for the Tellable, here is its home.
Speak and proclaim. More than ever
Things we can live with are falling away, for that
Which is oustingly taking their place is an imageless act.[1]

Christians and Muslims are faced with a similar challenge when they confront the reality of contemporary Europe: How can the sincere believer also participate fully in the public life of his or her nation as a citizen? In this essay I examine more closely the private and public identity of citizens in secular liberal democracies. More specifically, I am interested in a narrow question about the relationship between these two aspects of self-identity. Are they positively related: Does a secure personal (e.g., religious or cultural) identity facilitate trust of a political community? Or are they negatively related: Does a

strong personal identity preclude or at the very least make more difficult identification with the public life of a nation? Following from this enquiry I open up
a set of questions about the implications of this relationship for other citizens
(from another religion or no religion), for religious communities, and for the
state. At each stage I use arguments and sources that are general in their application. Although in some parts of this essay I examine the subject from the point
of view of Islam, I hope that the discussion will raise points that are immediately familiar to those of other beliefs and thus to a wider audience.[2]

Believers in Private, Citizens in Public

In modern secular democracies the public–private dichotomy is almost an article of faith. Its advocates will vigorously defend an individual's right to religion
in the private sphere while at the same time vigilantly guarding the public
sphere as a neutral religion-free zone. This idea influences not only politics but
also more generally our public sphere and common culture. The public sphere
and politics, it is argued, must be free of parochial religious bias. It must be
governed according to public reason, which will yield an outcome that all citizens can agree is valid despite their individual beliefs. These reason-based forms
of public debate are, in Michael Oakeshott's words, "the enemy of authority,
of the merely traditional, customary or habitual."[3] Thus "the rationalist is
essentially uneducable" in relation to issues of tradition and narrative because
they require from him or her "an inspiration which is regarded as the greatest
enemy of mankind."[4] Yet where is the space for faith in this analysis? Should
the sincere believer be satisfied with the relegation of the most critical aspect of
his or her self-understanding to the private sphere?

At first sight it seems unlikely that such a sharp dichotomy between the
public and private, this all-or-nothing approach to private and public identity,
is realistic. It is worth noticing that it is not just secular liberals who insist on
playing this zero-sum game. Advocates of religion make a similar mistake when
they insist that a private religious identity can be formed or can develop in
isolation from the secular world. Let me say something more about each of
these points to justify my conclusions.

Secular liberalism's insistence on the strict separation of the private sphere
(where individuals form and revise their conception of the good) and the public

sphere (which preserves neutrality between individuals) is well known. The assumption is that individuals are able to create and sustain a religious (or racial or cultural) identity in their private life, while at the same time maintaining a distinct identity in the public sphere as citizens. A neutral public sphere where citizens come together to use public reason (rather than religion or culture) as the basis for decision making is the crucial organizing concept. The assumption is that the strict separation of the public and the private can be maintained. In fact, it is an essential part of secular liberal politics that this duality is the precondition for justice. The public–private duality ensures the separation of the right and the good: The neutral public sphere provides the framework created through the grant of individual rights (to freedom of speech, religion, and association) that leaves citizens free not only to pursue but also—and critically—to revise their concept of the good in their private life. It is crucial for secular liberalism that each citizen has this option: that each citizen can revise his or her concept of the good life and the most fundamental aspects of his or her private identity over a period of time. There is an attractive vision of freedom, choice, and control that underlies contemporary secular liberalism. It is often tempting for those with a religious perspective to undertake a wholesale critique of liberalism, to argue that those who find themselves attracted to liberalism are deluded. Such an extreme reaction fails to acknowledge that there is an appealing vision of a "free person" that drives this particular ideology and its supportive ideas of human choice, control, and individual responsibility.[5]

Recent critiques of liberalism have highlighted the flaws in its private–public dichotomy. We owe a great debt to Marxist and feminist critiques for highlighting these points. More recently, postmodern scholarship and multiculturalism have forced us to notice that relegating important aspects of personal identity to the private sphere is not a plausible solution. This radical critique has perceptively highlighted the fact that individuals want certain aspects of their personal identity to be acknowledged and "recognized" in the public sphere. This recognition, it is argued, is not just a luxury: It is an important aspect of the well-being of individuals that they should see their most valued sense of self reflected and respected in the public sphere. This feature of contemporary liberal culture—the "politics of identity" issue—focuses attention on a number of recurring themes in contemporary political writing. Writers such as Joseph Raz, Charles Taylor, and Alasdair MacIntyre have all addressed these topics. Although there remain important differences between each of these writers, their work highlights a number of common concerns. These theorists reject an atomistic picture of individual freedom as radical detachment. Their work recognizes an important link between individual freedom and identity on the one hand, and social practices and community on the other. A number of consequences follow from these connections. First, we are forced to notice that an important source of the well-being and self-respect of individuals arises out of their sense of who they are through their identification with important beliefs, groups, and attachments. Second, where these beliefs, attachments, and groups are denigrated, this in turn undermines the sources of self-respect and well-being of the individual. Raz states this in terms of "alienation from society" and the "pivotal importance of self-respect to the well-being of people."[6]

The fact that important aspects of identity are formed "dialogically" and the resulting importance of respect and recognition make issues of identity and group membership important for the public sphere.[7] The link between recognition by others and individual well-being raises the stakes in the "politics of identity" debate. Charles Taylor, for example, argues that an important additional feature of the politics of identity is the idea that the failure to grant recognition, or the misrecognition of the other, is characterized as a harm that can cause damage to the well-being of the individual. In this second sense—as the recognition of identity—the argument moves the politics of identity debate from the private to the public sphere. If recognition by others is important for individual well-being, then the failure to grant recognition, reflecting back to an individual a demeaning picture of himself or the group from which he draws his sense of self, can be categorized as a serious matter. The failure to grant recognition has implications for individuals' well-being and autonomy.[8] Where the state and its institutions are implicated in creating and sustaining this distorted image, there is a strong case that the requirements of the demands of the contemporary politics of identity and recognition have been breached. Paul Ricouer makes a similar point in a way that has special resonance for understanding a private religious identity when he concludes that narrative is important for a meaningful sense of self.[9]

There is then, in some limited circumstances, a strong argument for the recognition of a private religious identity in the public sphere. Those who are religious will agree with this part of the analysis quite easily. Yet at the same time they must also accept the corollary of the fact that identities are formed dialogically. If this is the case, then the claim that individual believers in a secular democracy are able to isolate their religious identity from the wider world in which they live becomes more difficult to justify. It also seems to me to be highly improbable that this is a realistic position. Our public life, the public culture that we create, is not just a product of each individual action. The public culture in which we are born and within which we develop as individuals is also an essential condition for our human agency. In fact, to argue that public culture—our community—is an essential ingredient in the production of human agency is to draw on an ancient line of authority. It is essentially an Aristotelian claim to insist that outside society man cannot be truly human: outside society man is either beast or god. This has particular relevance for understanding the relationship between a private religious identity and identity as public citizens. Noticing the causal relationship between a private identity and the public culture in which it develops challenges the view that there is a neutral, objective, religious "point from nowhere" to which an individual can withdraw either in understanding their own sense of self or in analyzing the world. This claim to neutrality is, in my view, the mirror image of traditional liberalism's insistence that there can be a strict separation between the public and the private spheres.

It seems more likely that in secular, liberal democracies there is a complicated relationship between a private religious identity and our public identity as citizens. Even, and perhaps especially, in those cases where individuals turn to religion as a way of escaping and rejecting the modern secular world, they cannot escape being influenced by the reality of the times in which they live. This may be something to regret for those who turn to religion as an escape from reality. However, for others there is some solace in the way in which this analysis forces us to recognize the importance of the details and the hard surfaces of life as the essential context within which private religious identity operates. These hard facts about life—the reality of the social, economic, and political stratification of the societies in which we live—act as a constraint on the way in which private religious identity is formed and the way in which this religious identity can realistically manifest itself in the daily lives of believers.

Moreover, rather than being a matter of regret, there is much to be gained by insisting that a private religious identity must attend to the hard features of our daily lives. It is often assumed, by those for whom religious or spiritual values are of great importance, that a concern with social justice and the distribution of resources is part of our current malaise: that it reveals a concern with worldly matters, that it is an illusion to assume that our daily and practical lives are significant, and that what is required is a radical detachment from the things of the world. In many contexts I have great sympathy with this move, and given modern conditions, it is an understandable and important way of seeking proximity to God. However, I remain fiercely committed to the view that access to basic resources, how individuals are treated, and therefore their meaningful experiences in the real world are of critical importance. These are the key determinants of autonomy, well-being, and the development of individual personality that facilitate the incorporation of a complex balance of religious and human goods over a long life of experience and activity, thereby enabling moral and spiritual excellence.

My main argument in this part of the essay is that the claim, whether by religion or secularism, that there is a strict dichotomy between an individual's private and public life is unrealistic. One cannot help influencing the other. So, just as liberal secularism has a causal effect on the private identity of the believer, religion also shapes and influences the public social order of secular societies. Once we notice this more complicated causal relationship, a series of other questions open up for consideration. What is the relationship between these two sources of identity—private religion and public citizenship? Are they positively or negatively related? What are the consequences of this relationship?

Justice as Public and Private Virtue

Political justice, as a public virtue of the state and its citizens, is the same quality as the virtue of individual justice that resides in the innermost parts of the soul. A number of different traditions have argued that private and public virtue is a continuation of the same value. Important texts in Greek philosophy treat the political virtues of the citizen as a continuation of the virtue ethics of the individual. There is also a tradition within Christian (Aquinas) and Islamic (al-Ghazālī) thought that explicitly draws on these classical sources. This literature is well known, and it has recently been revived in the work of modern writers such as Alasdair MacIntyre who regret the way in which the private–public dichotomy of secular liberalism makes it impossible to maintain unity between private and public virtue. MacIntyre is perhaps the most compelling authority in this regard: He has persuasively argued that modernity makes it difficult to create and sustain a unity of virtue.[10] Individual virtues—trust, love, friendship, and justice—are prerequisites and a preparation for developing public civic virtues—public duties, an obligation to obey the law, and a sense of social justice. It follows that the capacity to form close relationships of trust and friendship in personal relationships, families, and communities facilitates the ability to realize grander civic virtues. One further consequence of the break between private and public virtue is a fragmentation of value and a sense of alienation of individuals from the public sphere.

If there is, as I argue, a positive relationship between private and public identity, then this leads us in a number of directions. First, we can conclude that the state must take seriously the private aspects of its citizens' identity. Moreover, policies that foster a stable private religious identity and sustain religious communities take on a greater significance, not only because they are intrinsically valuable but also because they can yield considerable advantages through creating stable and just public civic institutions. Policies of multicul-turalism, which involve the recognition and accommodation of religion in the public sphere, become easier to justify. Finally, those whose private identity draws on religion view themselves as having an important public role: to partici-pate in public life in order to advance the common good for all citizens. It gives these individuals deeper reasons to participate in the public sphere. It may also encourage them to see any compromise that they are required to make as a "principled compromise" for the higher goal of a common good rather than as a sign of defeat and an inevitable consequence of their alienation from the public sphere. At an institutional level each religious tradition—Christianity and Islam—may need to consider how it can develop its own resources to support the processes that enable its adherents to enter into a deeper engage-ment with the public sphere.

If there is a negative relationship between a private religious identity and certain public virtues of a good citizen, then we are led down a different path. We have to conclude that religion is a barrier to participation in the public sphere, that it interferes with a stable identity as equal citizens. This, it seems to me, is the path taken by those who maintain a strict division between religion and state. The recent French headscarf *(foulard)* case illustrates this point. In the context of the vicious wars of religion that were fought in Europe between established religion and the state, a settlement that insists on a strict separation between religion and state is understandable. Whether or not such an inflexible model is still required under the current conditions in Europe, where the influence of organized religion and its link with political power is in decline, is perhaps more open to debate.[11]

Conclusions about whether there is a positive or negative relationship between a private religious identity and a public identity as citizens will have important policy implications in all those European countries that have religious minorities. Some of these issues are discussed in the case studies from Bosnia, Malaysia, and Britain later in this book. In the next part of the essay I examine more closely one aspect of this discussion: what happens when a private religious identity comes into contact with a public sphere that is based on secular values.

Religion and the Public Sphere in Secular Democracies

One way of understanding the relationship between religion and a secular public sphere is to examine the distinctive contribution of a religious perspective. What is the public status of a religious perspective? A certain perspective—whether religious or secular—is a way of seeing the world. A religious perspective is a way of discerning, understanding, and grasping reality that is in some ways distinct from other—including secular—perspectives. Yet at the same time, there are important points at which a religious and secular perspective may overlap. It is often assumed that there is a necessary conflict between a religious and a secular perspective. This assumption of an inherent conflict is especially true in discussions of Islam and the modern world. I want to set out an alternative way of understanding this relationship by using the specific example of Islam and leaving it to other faiths to explore the subject in their own way. Analyzing the issues in this way reveals—in my view—that the assumption of a confrontation between Islam and the secular world is not always the appropriate starting point for discussions. It is sometimes more useful to explore the relationship between an Islamic and secular perspective rather than to seek to uncover a close identity or stark opposition between them. Clifford Geertz presents three categories that are part of a worldview that allow us to make useful comparisons and explore this relationship in more detail.[12]

First, the *commonsense perspective* is a "mode of seeing that is a simple acceptance of the world, its objects, and its processes as being just what they seem to be—what is sometimes called naïve realism—and of the pragmatic motive, the wish to act upon the world so as to bend it to one's practical purposes, to master it, or so far as that proves impossible, to adjust to it."[13]

Second, the *scientific perspective* accepts reality and leads us to a different approach. The scientific perspective moves beyond acceptance of reality and emphasizes a different set of techniques: deliberate doubt, the suspension of the pragmatic motive in favor of disinterested observation, an attempt to analyze the world according to formal relationships, and a focus on concepts rather than unchallenged facts backed by common sense.

Third, and finally, the *aesthetic perspective* involves another type of distinct response. Like the scientific approach it requires a move away from realism and practical interest. However, unlike the scientific approach, the aesthetic perspective encourages attention to appearance using a different set of techniques. For example, an aesthetic perspective will move beyond reason-based analysis and require the engagement of our senses and imagination in an explicit way. It will require not only intellectual but also emotional responses: that is, understanding the written word as used in poems, literature, and drama; attention to the visual impact of architecture, painting, and sculpture; and a sensitive appreciation of music.

In exploring the relation between Islam and the secular modern world we can ask ourselves two questions: Does Islam have anything distinctive to add to each of these perspectives? Is there anything that Islam can, if not absorb, then at the very least react to, and interpret, in the modern secular approach to each of these perspectives? It is worth distinguishing a strong and a weak thesis at this point. The weak thesis would claim that it is possible to have a dialogue and exchange—that there are points of contact—between Islam, Muslims, and the modern world. The strong thesis would suggest that a deeper relationship is not only possible but also—and especially if one accepts some of the conclusions about the relationship between private and public identity—unavoidable. I have not reached a conclusion about which thesis is more probable. For the purposes of this essay it is not important for me to take sides. I do not want to provide a conclusive or definitive answer to these issues. Rather, I want to explore tentatively some points of contact between Islam and the secular modern world.

Once we approach the issue in this way it becomes clear that Islam can modify, adapt, and supplement some of the claims of a commonsense, scientific, and aesthetic perspective. In this way, rather than an inevitable confrontation, there is the possibility of a genuine interaction and dialogue between these seemingly opposite worldviews. Islam can accept the pragmatism and realism of the commonsense perspective. At the same time, it forces a movement beyond the realities of our everyday life to wider ideas and images that correct and complete them. Islam, like the scientific perspective, questions everyday realities. It can accept most of the methods and techniques of a scientific approach to uncovering the truth. However, it does so not out of institutionalized skepticism that dissolves the reality of the world in probabilities and hypothesis but in terms of what it takes to be wider truths. Moreover, its techniques are not limited to a radical detachment of scientific ideas from other systems such as ethics and concern for the environment.[14]

Attention to art and the use of imagination as a guide to the truth are common features of both the aesthetic and Islamic perspectives. For Muslims, a close attention to beauty in the natural world and artistic creation can be understood as a kind of freedom: It allows a movement away from reality as expressed within the commonsense and scientific perspectives toward more transcendent truths. Contemplation of the natural world and art also renews the ability to see and respond to these truths. There is within the Islamic tradition a well-established and deep connection between religious truths and beauty. Muslims comfortably endorse Keats's famous remark: "What the imagination seizes as beauty must be the truth."

Points of coalescence between an Islamic perspective and what we have identified as modern secular approaches are not just abstract possibilities. Islamic civilization has displayed a sober understanding of the truths about the world. Traditionally Muslims are advised to adjust to realities about the world in which they live with patience and a quiet faith. They are encouraged to believe that "all is right with the believer," "God is good, beauty and truth," "humanity is created in a state of intrinsic purity and goodness," and "this is the best of all possible worlds." Islam's ability to generate the most outstanding contributions in all fields of science, mathematics, physics, astronomy, and medicine is also well known. It is perhaps worth pointing out that these advances were never, and should not be claimed to be, the exclusive property of Islam or Muslims. This knowledge is best understood as the product of a certain community of thinkers, both Muslims and non-Muslims working together. What is significant is that Islamic civilization was able to create an environment in which Muslims along with non-Muslims were encouraged to pursue scientific enquiry that generated some outstanding results. Finally, it is well known that Islam has made an outstanding contribution in art. This contribution includes architecture, literature, and poetry in all the languages of Islam, calligraphy, art, and music across a vast temporal and geographical space. All these achievements are a testimony to Islam's ability to generate the imagination toward beauty.

Modernity's Critiques of Islam

Of course Muslims will not find any of this analysis difficult to accept. What they will find more troublesome is the claim that they should be more open to secularism. They will object to the argument that a secular perspective may have something valuable to say to them. Does a secular perspective have any contribution to make to Islam? Of course allowing a deeper dialogue gives secularism an opportunity to offer a critique of Islam. Would such a critique be an unacceptable threat to Islam and Muslims? Muslims will want to stress that there is a discernable essence to Islam that cannot be challenged. Yet it is possible to accept this claim without falling into the error of a strict essentialism that claims that Islam has an "all or nothing" monolithic structure. Islam—the Muslim community—like any complex system of ideas and groups contains not just one but a plurality of ideas and arguments. Some of these ideas and voices have been and are backed by existing power structures while others are relatively silent, do not have access to public space, and are struggling for recognition. To accept this sophistication, breadth, and depth within Islam is not to collapse into unacceptable social constructivism. Once this complexity within Islam and Muslim communities is accepted, the possibility of a legitimate place for criticism by "outsiders" opens up. This is exactly the space where "outsiders," those from another religion or with a secular perspective, can play a pivotal role. International conflicts and the war on terror have meant that Islam has been uniquely associated with irrationality and violence, with the consequence of a growing anti-Muslim prejudice that can cause significant harm to individuals and communities. As well as offering a critique, it is important for non-Muslims also to show solidarity with Muslims during this difficult period in history. However, Muslims should not seek the reification of Islam by outsiders. An uncritical and automatic grant of approval is not what is required: This can sometimes collapse into condescension rather than solidarity. The challenge for outsiders, for anyone offering a critique of Islam and Muslim communities, is to strike a balance between showing solidarity for Muslims and maintaining an authentic critical perspective.

A particularly British example illustrates the willingness of secular commentators to undertake exactly this task. Seumas Milne, writing in the *Guardian*, suggests that this balance is possible. He argues that existing political movements can form alliances with religious groups such as Muslims without compromising a critical stance on issues such as gender and sexuality.[15] His colleague Polly Toynbee, often and unfairly portrayed as being hostile toward Islam, is more skeptical. She poses the dilemma faced by liberal democrats in its most vivid form: "Atheists, feminists and anti-racists are paralysed by Islam. Whichever way they turn, they find themselves at risk of alliances with undesirables of every nasty hue." She quite rightly and perceptively insists that "Muslims must also accept the right of others to criticise their religion without smearing any critic as racist."[16]

Encouraging criticism and safeguarding free speech is obviously important to liberal democrats. It is also in the interests of Muslims to ensure that contemporary critics are not "paralysed by Islam," as Toynbee suggests. One of the most valuable contributions that outsiders can make is to "hold the line" in their analysis of Muslim communities. Commentators such as Toynbee often provide the most prescient critique of Muslim communities. Insiders can turn to this critique as a precious source of information and ideas. It is a strongly held belief among Muslims that Islam contains within it the resources to allow them to challenge injustice and oppression within their own communities. However, this belief should not prevent them from appropriating legitimate arguments from outside their own tradition, using the experience of other political movements as a precious source of ideas and experience, and making demands for dignity by citing successful examples from other traditions. Criticism of Muslim communities is not the problem. What is lamentable is the way in which constructive skepticism often collapses into a less coherent position: the view that Muslims must shed all their religious affiliations before they can be considered legitimate partners in public debate. This is a significant barrier to Muslims' establishing intellectual and political alliances that would assist them in challenging injustice within their own communities.

The failure to encourage an exchange of ideas and alliances in public life that transcends difference, and the resulting alignment of the public sphere and politics along the lines of race, culture, and religion, is one of the more damaging by-products of the public recognition of private identity. This shift entrenches and emphasizes differences that are often irrelevant, which in turn contributes to the fragmentation of our public sphere. One criterion—race, religion, or culture—cannot provide a definitive marker in all contexts. A single aspect of personal identity should not be allowed to predetermine the vast range of possibilities for public speech and action open to minorities such as Muslims. Participation in the public sphere, modern politics, and multiculturalism require a nuanced and sophisticated version of social and political equality: one in which race and religion are restructured in conjunction with other valid and urgent categories such as international justice, gender, and class. Muslims should reevaluate the terms of their involvement in the public sphere of their individual countries to take account of a full spectrum of issues if they are to move toward meaningful forms of participation. They should intervene to support the common good for all citizens. Islam is not—and never was—a ghetto for parochial religious bias. There is also some work to be done in the field of secular approaches to legitimate public participation. Public institutions in secular liberal democracies need to reach out to excluded and marginalized groups such as Muslims. They may also need to relinquish some of their tighter disciplines about what constitutes a legitimate contribution to public debate and participation, in favor of greater plurality in the realm of ideas and policies and also in fields such as science and art.

If Islam is to be a credible voice in the modern secular world then it must be able to respond to these hard facts of life—economic, social, and political—in an intelligent way. Obviously Islam, like all other traditional religions, has an immense amount to learn from modern science. Yet at the same time, it can also make an important contribution to a contemporary scientific perspective by emphasizing that the techniques of modern science, although invaluable, need to pay greater attention to ethics and the environment. Even in the sphere of aesthetics—which many argue is the most powerful illustration of the corruption of the modern world—there is something to learn as well as contribute.

The modern secular world produces some outstanding cultural products that provide an invaluable resource. One recent example is the work of Philip Pullman, whose recent trilogy, *His Dark Materials*, is a powerful testimony to the fact that a deeply secular, and at times antireligious, writer can capture and express important religious truths. Pullman, through his characters and dramatic narrative, expresses the virtues of compassion and justice, love and friendship, and displays a greater discernment of "religious" truths than many contemporary religious writers. Works of art are the product of individuals. Of course, the beliefs of these individuals are critical influences on their work. These individuals may not have a formal religious perspective, they may be explicitly hostile to religion, or they may be writing about purely secular matters. However, this does not stop them or modern secular art from capturing essential truths that are invaluable to religious traditions.

On all these fronts—the political, social, and economic; the scientific; and the aesthetic—Islam can make a contribution. Also, and more controversially, it has something to gain by opening itself up to the modern secular world. Of course, there are risks in such an intimate encounter. The chief victim is certainty, as the secure sense of reality that Muslims experience in their private identity is challenged by their public experience. Is this a bad thing? Perhaps, but only if you think that the function of a private religious identity is to give you access to absolute truth by eliminating shades of gray. There are some aspects of this claim to absolute certainty in all religions. For example, Islam tells us that there are certain universal human goods such as the *maqāṣid* (human goals) of al-Ghazālī's legal and political theory: life, family, knowledge, religion, and property. Islam also guides us to universal ethical values and emotions: that is, compassion and mercy, truth and justice. Islamic law delineates how these goals and values can be inculcated in a daily life; it even resolves some conflicts between goods and values for Muslims by acting as a guide to individual choice. All of these resources call into question modern secularism's fatal error: the slide into subjectivism. However, this insistence on objective values and truth does not eliminate the fact of uncertainty. A private religious identity in the modern secular world cannot generate one right answer that can respond to all difficult questions. My suspicion is that this is not just a fact about the modern world but is better understood as an aspect of the human condition.

Nevertheless, what is distinctive about the modern condition is that it has removed the security of unalterable "horizons of significance" and made disbelief a plausible and widely endorsed option. This does provide a more significant challenge to individual private religious belief. In the face of this skepticism, what is needed is the humility to recognize that devout believers—sincere Muslims—like many other citizens, will experience moments of confusion. There will always be those unsettling episodes where one's moral insights are inadequate to explain one's moral experience. These moments of ethical confusion are a fact for human beings. We will always face ethical conflicts; we cannot avoid paradox. This will be especially true where religion coexists with a modern secular perspective that crowds out the public space for unshakeable faith. Modernity leaves all believers, including Muslims, with no choice but to accept these conflicts and to learn to think in what Robert Graves calls "broken images."[17]

Islam's Critique of the Modern World

Islam has, as noted earlier, something to contribute to the commonsense, scientific, and aesthetic perspectives. The Islamic intellectual tradition and its civilization have made, and can continue to make, an outstanding contribution in all these categories. The distinctive offering of Islam, however, does not lie in the way in which it overlaps with the secular perspective. Islam's unique quality lies in its ability to reveal the "spiritual limits" of the modern condition. There is no conflict or uncertainty about this issue: Islam gives unequivocal and crystal clear priority to the centrality of religious observance and spirituality. Ritual prayer, which is conducted five times a day and which gives a central place to the sacred liturgy of Islam, has a particular significance in this context. Other rituals such as fasting, alms giving, and pilgrimage, as well as supererogatory acts such as the remembrance of God, are also of fundamental importance. These sacred acts are motivated by private belief, but they are also public: They are performed and observable by others in the public world. For Muslims, they are the alpha and the omega of their faith. It is in sacred ritual, in the acts of consecrated behavior, that the distinctive and unique perspective that Islam brings to bear on the world and the reality of the modern secular world meet.

In ritual, a world that is perceived, understood, and imagined by Muslims is made real. Ritual uses the symbolic act and gesture to fuse the world that is lived and the world that is imagined. It is in sacred ritual that these are transformed into the same world.[18] It is through these concrete acts of religious observance that Islam—and the religious conviction of individual Muslims—makes its most astonishing mark on the modern secular world.

To stress the importance of ritual is not to imply that Muslim women or men can live within a system of religious observance or symbols for the whole of their lives. Hence the earlier insistence on understanding the hard facts—social, economic, political—of life as an essential prerequisite for understanding the place of religion. The majority of Muslims live within this sacred space for only some brief moments of their life. The everyday world of common objects and practical acts is the paramount reality of their human experience. This is not a startling fact for Muslims, who are comfortable with the idea that their rituals are a preparation for their everyday life. The dispositions of character and personality that ritual induces in Muslims' private lives have their most important impact outside the world of religious symbols. These dispositions reflect back and influence the perceptions of Muslims when they seek to understand the established modern secular world. Moreover, as I have argued, these aspects influence the self-identity of Muslims as public citizens.

There is, then, for Muslims a movement back and forth between the religious perspective and the commonsense everyday perspective. The religious belief that they experience in moments of ritual and religious observance, which transports them to another mode of existence, continues into their everyday existence. In this way the experience within private ritual influences the public identity of Muslims in the modern world in critical ways. Private ritual also links individual Muslims to the unfolding of human history beyond the current conditions of modernity. Within their rituals Muslims use set actions that date back to the first Muslims and fixed language from the Qur'anic text in Arabic; ritual prayer links Muslims to a narrative tradition beyond their personal history to an unfolding of human history in the Qur'an. This narrative history places Muslims as part of the monotheistic tradition of Judaism, Christianity, and Islam. Observable acts of ritual performed by Muslims create the startling link between two worlds: the reality of Islam and the modern secular world. It is exactly in this space, at this point of contact, that Muslims have something truly distinctive to offer the modern secular world.

This is not a critique, a wholesale rejection of all the products of modernity, or disillusion. From this perspective, Islam is well placed to offer a critique of the "spiritual" limits of a public sphere preoccupied with politics and individual fulfillment. This invaluable contribution should not, however, collapse into a wholesale critique of modernity. What is needed instead is a patient and insistent reminder of some basic and eternal truths that are the essence of Islam but that have been inverted in our current civilization, with its preoccupation with politics and work, production and consumption. Most important is the stark truth of monotheism, of the reality of one God, that is above all else the constant theme of the Qur'an. Islam can also offer a picture of the "concept of the person" that is a dramatic challenge to modern ideas of the person as merely voter, worker, and consumer. In a vivid contrast to this vision, Islam insists that women and men are created in dignity with an inherent capacity for goodness. Islam can also challenge modernity's slide into subjectivism by affirming the objective universal values that permeate the whole of its ethical structure— compassion and mercy, justice and truth—as well as the human goods—family, friendship, and knowledge—that are the ultimate goals of all human cooperation. In many cases this critique will not reveal something new: It is better understood as the more modest but essential work of reflecting back to individuals the values that underlie their most cherished assumptions.

The proper image for this activity is not one borrowed from science: the discovery and creation of a brave new world. Rather, this mission is more like archaeology: recovering, recognizing, and remembering virtues and goods that will be immediately familiar to individuals; adding them to the pool of ideas available in the public sphere; and providing a language that allows them to be expressed. This last task of articulacy of values is the most critical: We urgently need to develop a greater articulacy, to the self and in dialogue with others, of values that may have become corrupted or muted in recent times.[19] In all these ways Islam contains within it resources that offer a radical critique of modernity's concept of the person, its ambition for relationships between persons and its vision about the proper ends of social life.

Replacing what Rilke has called the "imageless act" haunting modernity cannot be done without operating in the public world. It must be undertaken by attending to the reality of the hard facts of life and by a sober acceptance of the modern secular world. Muslims have a distinct perspective to communicate, but this cannot be done through acts of wholesale and abstract rejection.

Rather, the challenge is to bring a unique perspective, developed in the most intimate private acts of ritual, to bear upon the reality of the modern world. Rilke's *Ninth Elegy* reminds us of the attitude when performing this supremely delicate task:

> *Praise this world to the Angel, not the untellable: you*
> *Can't impress him with the splendor you've felt; in the cosmos*
> *Where he more feelingly feels you're only a novice. So show him some simple thing.*

There is a significant cost in any move from a stable religious experience in the private sphere to functioning as full citizens in public life. Muslims, like many other people, are faced with a public order in the modern world that fails to reflect, and often contradicts, their deepest and most passionate beliefs. Muslims who seek to intervene in the public sphere will face insuperable difficulties. Many may prefer to withdraw from public life to guard their faith. This is a legitimate response to modernity: It is a mistake to assume that all individuals must participate in public life to lead a life of religious and human value. Islam does not assume that the grand heroic virtues can only be realized through public and political acts. In fact, many of the most important values of Islam, such as compassion and mercy, can be realized within the private and domestic sphere. Those Muslims who choose to follow a different path, to move out of the private sphere and intervene in the modern world, will face a different set of questions. They will need to ask themselves whether they are willing to make sacrifices to their individual sense of certainty and private self-identity in order to challenge some of the most pernicious errors of modern secularism. This need not necessarily be a negative process. Facing the reality of the public world in which they live provides Muslims with some significant opportunities if they can prevent the unnecessary compromise of their identity. This in turn can force them to focus on the present to avoid a preoccupation with a perfect future that often prevents them from seeing and learning from the reality that is in front of them.

Maintaining this "porous" attitude to present reality can make Muslims more open to questions about how they can be available to transform themselves. However, there can be no way of avoiding the facts that in confronting the modern secular world Muslims will need to reconcile their private faith with public action and that this will challenge their sense of reality and may in some cases require them to compromise cherished beliefs. Muslims often see compromise along these lines as a defeat that is forced on them and a confirmation of their powerlessness in the modern world. This attitude ignores the way in which the Islamic intellectual tradition contains considerable resources for developing a "principled compromise" that may be a legitimate response to modernity. Conflict between public life and private belief and the need for a "principled compromise" is especially difficult for Muslims for whom the theological doctrine of unity (*tawḥīd*) is of great importance. This focus on unity leads to a preference that all sources of normative authority in the lives of individual Muslims should point in the same direction. This in turn encourages Muslims to search for coherence in all aspects of their lives as part of their quest for spiritual perfection and proximity to God. The public order that faces Muslims in the modern world makes such a high degree of coherence impossible.

Muslims operating in public life will have to develop skills rather like those of an alchemist: the ability to recognize and maintain fine distinctions between those precious activities and relations with which there should be engagement and struggle, and those areas of contemporary life that need to be rejected or endured in silence. Such a Herculean task invariably introduces the prospect of conflict, remorse, and anguish. It is therefore easy to understand why a strategy of self-sufficiency and closure from the world seems preferable and why many Muslims, along with many other people, develop a distaste for the times in which they live. The result is a state of disengagement with public life and disenchantment with the social world. Muslims need to resist such pessimism. They need to constantly nudge back into the public perspective their vision of the inherent dignity of persons in the face of a modern public culture that often reduces human beings to mere workers and consumers. They need to act to create and sustain a community in which all people, Muslims and non-Muslims, can realize the most fundamental goods and virtues in their daily lives.

This important work for Muslims is captured most vividly by Rilke in his *Ninth Elegy*:

> *Here is the time for the Tellable, here is its home.*
> *Speak and proclaim. More than ever*
> *things we can live with are falling away, for that*
> *which is oustingly taking their place is an imageless act.*

Replacing the imageless act is the great contribution that Muslims can make if they can find the courage to move out of the safety of being "believers in private" and participate fully in secular liberal democracies as "citizens in public." Muslims need to maintain a fine balance between optimistic intervention in support of their vision of the concept of the person and the common good for all people, while at the same time being realistic about the substantial obstacles that they face in communicating the truth about Islam. Once we move away from crude assumptions of a clash between civilizations—and the specter of an inherent conflict between Islam and the modern world—a wider range of possibilities becomes clear. It becomes easier to imagine not only the way in which Islam can adjust itself to the reality of the modern world but also the myriad of ways in which it can make an invaluable contribution to the times in which we live. There are, in my view, good reasons to believe that Islam will not only survive but also—perhaps surprisingly for some—flourish in the modern secular world.

Christian Faith and National Belonging

ح٥

Michael Nazir-Ali

T he origins of Christian attitudes to the state are found in the Bible. Already in ancient Israel, the emergence of the monarchy was reluctantly recognized as necessary (maybe even as a necessary evil), and the rights and duties of kingship were prescribed (1 Sam. 8–10). The stories about Nathan and David and Elijah and Ahab show us that the monarchy was not regarded as absolute but as accountable to the laws of God (2 Sam. 12; 1 Kings 21). During their period of exile in Babylon, the Jewish people were told to work for and pray for the well-being of the place to which they had been exiled (Jer. 29:7). The general situation in the Older Testament, with regard to foreign rulers, is to respect them and even serve them, provided that such respect and service do not in any way compromise the duty and worship owed to God alone.[20] With Cyrus the Persian, however, there is already a development in that he is regarded as the Lord's anointed in the fulfillment of the divine plan for the return of the exiles from Babylon (Isa. 45:1–2).

At the time of Jesus, the Jewish people paid taxes to the Roman and other authorities. The *censum,* or poll tax, which was universally hated but paid nevertheless, and the taxes levied by the Herodian rulers are examples of such payment. In the context of the *censum,* Jesus's teaching about rendering to Caesar what is his and to God what properly belongs to God indicates the scope of obedience to temporal rulers (Mark 12:13–17 and parallels). There is an obligation to pay for the protection and the amenities provided, but in such a way and to such an extent that the rights of God are not usurped and divine sovereignty is not compromised.[21] It seems that after the destruction of the temple in AD 70, the tax for the upkeep of the temple was transferred to the

Roman authorities, who used it for the cult of Jupiter. The continued payment of this tax exempted the Jews from active participation in the imperial cult but required, to some extent, an implicit recognition of it. It seems that at least some Christians wanted to continue belonging to the synagogue precisely so that they could pay the tax and thus avoid ascribing divine honors to the emperor. Their expulsion from the synagogues at the same time as Domitian's demand that he should be worshipped as *dominus et deus* exposed them to the particular persecution that is referred to in the Apocalypse of St. John.[22]

Before the full force of the Neronian persecution was felt by the Christians, Paul's experience of the Pax Romana led him to the positive view of imperial power that we find in Romans 13: God is the fount of all authority, and the authority of earthly rulers is derived from God. Human government is an aspect of the divine ordering of creation and is necessary for the common good. It is appropriate, therefore, for Christians to obey the laws of the state, to pay all taxes due to it, and to give proper respect to the authorities.

The principles enunciated in a time of peace held, however, even on the eve of and during a fiery persecution. The First Letter of Peter, which was probably written even as the persecution of Nero was breaking out, echoes much of what is found in St. Paul's letter to the Romans. There are admittedly some differences that arise perhaps from the context: The emphasis now is not on the divine ordering of societies but on the various human forms in which such ordering is expressed. Christians are told, nevertheless, to submit to "every human institution" that exists to promote human welfare and for the punishment of those who would harm it (1 Pet. 2:13–17).

There is always, however, a caveat, first expressed by Peter and the other apostles at the very beginning of their confrontation with the Jewish authorities: that they must obey God rather than human beings (Acts 5:29). Human authorities are to be obeyed as long as they act in accordance with their mandate and do not trespass on what is God's will for his creation. If they do, for example, by restricting people's freedom to respond to the love of God in confession of belief and worship, they are to be resisted. "Caesar" can certainly transgress the limits of his jurisdiction by claiming divine honors and by waging war against the saints. St. Paul could see this happening if the restraining hand of the law was withdrawn (2 Thess. 2:6–7), and, for Augustine, if justice is removed, the state simply becomes a system of legalized robbery.[23] The idea that rulers are subject to the law of God and not above it has had important consequences in constitutional history and in making rulers subject to the law that gives them authority to govern but also protects those who are governed.[24]

By the time of Domitian, the imperial cult had become so oppressive for Christians that the wise magistrate of the letter to the Romans becomes the beast from the abyss who wages war on God's people in the last book of the Bible, the Revelation of St. John the Divine (Rev. 13). During the second and third centuries AD, there were periods of peace for the church but also periods of violent persecution. During this time, Christians developed ways of explaining their faith to the pagan world around them, especially to those in authority, and of demanding justice from them. They were also keen to assure their rulers that they prayed for them regularly—as, of course, we do today. Walter Wink and Lesslie Newbigin remind us that the victory over the imperial system was not won by seizing the levers of power. It was won when those about to be martyred knelt down and prayed for the emperor.[25] The "apology" became a favorite form of doing these things, and although it was often addressed to those who wielded political and military power, sometimes it was more general.[26]

Much is known about the persecution of Christians throughout the Roman Empire, but there was persecution elsewhere as well, especially within the domains of the other superpower of the time, the Persian Empire. The fifth century Greek historian Sozomen, writing about the persecutions of the previous century in the Persian Empire, tells us that there were at least sixteen thousand martyrs. He is well aware that there may have been others.[27]

The edicts of toleration, when they came in the two empires, had somewhat different results. The edicts of Yazdgard in 410 AD recognized the Christians as a valid community in the land. Its affairs were organized on the basis of the now well-known millet system, which survived into Islamic times and was used by the Ottomans right up to the modern period. As a millet, Christians had rights and obligations in relation to the empire, but they remained a distinct community within it. The Edict of Milan, on the other hand, a century earlier, led eventually to the emergence of the *Corpus Christianum*, the idea that, while church and state were distinct societies, they were united in one commonwealth and manifested different aspects of it. In Byzantium, the emperor became the dominant partner in this alliance, whereas in the West the Middle Ages were marked by claims of the papacy to be dominant.[28] The Persian and Roman models offer two perspectives on being the church vis-à-vis the state. In the former, Christians are a distinct but tolerated community who are able to make a limited contribution to the empire in which they are set. In the latter, there is virtual identification between empire and church. In the course of history the Byzantine model of the godly king or emperor who had jurisdiction in both church and state became more and more attractive to emerging monarchies in western Europe and is at the basis of the various settlements that were concluded at the time of the Reformation.[29]

The eastern and western parts of the Roman Empire are not, of course, the only examples of the *Corpus Christianum*: Already toward the end of the third century the nation of Armenia had become the first to be officially Christian, and Ethiopia became a Christian empire during the fifth century at the latest. By contrast, some churches, such as the Coptic Orthodox and the Syrian Jacobites, have nearly always existed as distinct communities within polities that have often been hostile to them. In India, the rulers were not always hostile, but the ancient churches there were always a clear minority.

Throughout the story of the church there have been groups of Christians, such as the Lollards, the Hussites, and the Waldensians, who have emphasized the nature of the church as a distinct and gathered community that does not need the arm of civil authority to give it special protection and that cannot be identified with natural groupings, whether ethnic or territorial. The Reformation period gave such groups great encouragement so that some emerged from the shadows and new ones came into existence. Although they differed markedly from one another and were not free of conflict even within themselves, they were characterized by a certain family resemblance. They believed in the pure congregation or society of saints who were called out of the world and maintained a distinctive lifestyle that often included refusal of military service, pacifism, and extreme simplicity. They rejected both the worldliness of contemporary Roman Catholicism and the Erastianism of the "mainstream" Reformation churches. Because of this, they were sometimes persecuted on all sides.[30]

Even within the so-called mainstream, however, there were groups who wanted their church to be more like the New Testament churches and therefore less aligned to the state, however "Christian" the latter claimed to be. There were others who had serious reservations about the Erastian aspect of church–state relations in many parts of Europe and yet others who could see that the divided state of the Christian churches would remain unless the link with the state was somehow loosened. The Puritans in the Church of England, for example, wanted the Reformation to continue and were determined to resist the monarch and the bishops in this matter. Their legacy remains an important one in the Anglican Communion today. The Non-Jurors emerged as a party that resisted the king because they believed in the divine right of monarchs. Having taken the oath of allegiance to the exiled James II, they refused to take one to the newly arrived William and Mary. Those who refused included the archbishop of Canterbury, eight other bishops, and four hundred clergy. The Non-Jurors were active in liturgical development, in ecumenism (especially in relation to the Orthodox) and in the fostering of spirituality. For our purposes, however, their most important characteristic was a high conception of the church as a spiritual society with its own laws that was held alongside an equally high view of the monarchy and of the obedience due to it.

It was this principle that they bequeathed to the Tractarians and that was at stake in the attempt by the Whig government in the 1830s to suppress a number of bishoprics in Ireland. The question was not whether the bishoprics ought to be suppressed but whether the government should be acting in a matter that was proper to the church. John Keble's sermon on "National Apostasy" in 1833 tackled this issue and is generally regarded as the beginning of the Catholic revival in the Church of England.[31] This revival initiated fresh ways of thinking about the relationship between church and state.

David Nicholls has discerned two main tendencies in Anglican Catholic thought: the incarnationalist and the redemptionist. The incarnationalist approach he regards as optimistic and gradualist: the Kingdom of God comes slowly, silently, and peacefully—as the mighty are lowered from their seats, this is so gently done that they do not feel the bump when they hit the ground! Against this tendency are the redemptionists. Although they too regard the Incarnation as important, they also emphasize the Cross where there is a decisive battle between Good and Evil. While creation, for them, is fundamentally good, they take due account of the pervasive effects of the Fall, particularly on the social, economic, and political structures of human society. Although they are prepared to work with these structures, they refuse to sacralize them and, most importantly, refuse to confuse the church with them. Both Nicholls and Dr. Rowan Williams, now archbishop of Canterbury, refer in this respect to the work of John Neville Figgis.[32] Figgis regarded the state as an "association of associations" but an association that had the power to balance the claims and order the relations of its constitutive parts. Within such a structure, the church can maintain its distinct witness to the Gospel that continually challenges the foundations on which the kingdoms of this world are built. It is interesting, in this connection, to note that Dr. Williams refers to Figgis in the context of the need to take liberation theologies seriously—theologies that, at the very least, oblige us to analyze patterns of domination and deprivation as obstacles to the transformation offered by the Gospel. A theological critique of our social and political context implies a Christian community that has an understanding of distinctiveness, as well as of belonging, in the situation in which it finds itself.

Both Williams and Nicholls are aware of the questions raised by Figgis's work: the extent to which societies are providentially ordered for the sake of the common good, for instance, and also the basis for Christian cooperation with the secular organs of the state in matters of justice, compassion, and access.

Such views of church–state relationships leave little room for coercion on either side: The state must respect the proper autonomy of the church, except where the liberty and welfare of others may be involved, and the church must, as Figgis urged, recognize a proper sphere for the state to govern. What else can we say of this relationship? There can be what Nicholls somewhat dismissively calls "the influencing of society." This is hardly revolutionary, and certainly melioristic, but often effective nevertheless. There can also be "prophetic witness" over and against society, toward which Nicholls would be more sympathetic, and there can be "struggle" on behalf of those who are powerless, excluded, and deprived. It is, of course, possible to imagine not only the influencing of society but also prophetic witness and even struggle taking place both outside and within the councils of state, if the church is afforded a voice there.

Even where there is a formal separation of church and state, however, we find that forms of government and structures of state can be formatively influenced by a religious tradition. The American Declaration of Independence and the subsequent constitutional history of the United States amply bear this out.[33] In Europe and elsewhere—for example, Armenia and Ethiopia as examples of "old" Christendoms, as well as the Philippines in Asia and many states in modern Africa—there has been and continues to be a more direct link between Christianity and constitutional arrangements. Law, moreover, if it is to have moral and not merely coercive force, must be grounded in a spiritual and moral tradition on which it can also draw in the course of its development. No doubt there are analogues to these matters in the world of Islam that our Muslim friends will be able to discuss, but of course a developmental view of the relation between law and religion cannot be simply about the adoption of legal codes framed in a different age for very different purposes.

This brings me to questions of dialogue and reciprocity. We need to arrive at a point where we can frankly acknowledge not only the historical position of Islam or Christianity vis-à-vis constitutional and legal arrangements in various countries but also their influence in the present and for the future. Such an acknowledgment would deliver us from the false hopes associated with allegedly secular politics. We will still need to ask, however, in a dialogical context, how people of other faiths, and of none, can creatively contribute in a social and political situation that has largely been formed under the influence of a particular tradition. We will also need to ensure that the commitment to freedoms of expression and of worship and to participation in political, economic, and social life in one context is also expected of other contexts. Those engaged in dialogue have committed themselves to such basic freedoms and access to community life for all in every place, and particularly where they have influence.

We know that St. Paul used his Roman citizenship to good effect in the course of his missionary work (Acts 16:37–39, 22:25–29), whereas the First Letter of St. Peter describes Christians as strangers and exiles in this world (1 Pet. 2:11). This tension between belonging and not belonging, between being citizens and yet exiles in the present order, has remained in Christian thinking about the relationship between faith and nation, faith and ethnicity, and faith and culture. It is best summed up in a second- or third-century letter written to an enquirer, the so-called Epistle to Diognetus. The writer describes Christians in this way:

> They dwell in their own countries but as strangers. They share all things as citizens and suffer all things as foreigners. Every foreign country is their home and their own country is foreign to them. They marry like everyone else and have children but they do not expose their offspring. They share their table with others but not the marriage bed. Their lot is to be in the flesh, yet they do not live according to the flesh. They pass their time on earth but their citizenship is in heaven. They obey the appointed laws but surpass them in their own lives. They love everyone but are persecuted by everyone. They are unknown and are condemned. They are put to death and gain life. Although they are poor, they make many rich. They have nothing and yet they have everything. They are dishonoured but are glorified in their dishonour. They are regarded as evil but are justified. They

are abused but they bless. They are insulted and they honour. When they do good and are called evil, they rejoice as those receiving life.[34]

The tension cannot easily be resolved, and we have to live with it creatively—both belonging and not belonging, as part of society and yet strangers to some of its standards and values, as citizens but also as exiles.

Faith and National Identity of Catholics in Bosnia-Herzegovina

Mato Zovkic

I would like to draw attention to some delicate problems of religious identity and national loyalty from the point of view of religious and ethnic communities in my own country of Bosnia-Herzegovina. Religious identity surpasses the boundaries of an ethnic group or country, but in this region, where Catholicism, Orthodoxy, Islam, and Judaism have been meeting for centuries, ethnic and religious identity mostly coincide.

What Nationality, What Kind of Loyalty?

On March 1, 1992, the democratically elected government of Bosnia-Herzegovina organized a referendum in which citizens were asked to decide whether they wanted to remain within a truncated Yugoslavia or to become a new, independent country. The Catholic bishops in their pastoral letter encouraged their flock to participate in the referendum and to give their voices to independence. A majority of citizens did take part in voting and voted for independence. After nearly four years of war, which we Croats-Catholics and Bosniacs-Muslims consider as aggression while our fellow citizens who are Serbs-Orthodox call it a civil war, the present-day Bosnia-Herzegovina, with its two entities, was created through the Dayton Agreements. Webster's Dictionary defines a nation as a "body of people, associated with a particular territory, that is sufficiently conscious of its unity to seek or possess a government peculiarly its own." In Western democracies, the nation is a state where all citizens share a national identity, despite many individual and group identities within the same nation.

After Dayton, Bosnia-Herzegovina is hardly a nation with such a meaning, because we still disagree on what kind of state we want. Bosnia-Herzegovina is an internationally recognized country where citizens of three ethnic communities share common needs for jobs and for tolerant neighborly relations but do not share the same dream of statehood or nationhood.

Let me give an example. Three members of Parliament, of the Socialist Party, recently made a draft of a law on public holidays. Their draft was taken into consideration by the respective Commission of Parliament, and on May 11, 2005, a public discussion of the draft took place in the Parliament building. Representatives of the churches and religious communities were invited to take part in that discussion. I was asked to attend that meeting by the Catholic archbishop of Sarajevo. In the interventions made, one could see the ethnicity of the speakers. Bosniac-Muslim speakers, including the delegate of the Muslim community, were content with the draft text. The Croat delegates fundamentally advocated the draft text but proposed some changes. There was a vague proposal on the religious feasts of Muslims and Christians that would be recognized by the new law as public holidays—I intervened in this section. Six speakers, all ethnic Serbs, strongly rejected the whole draft. They insisted that the Serbs of Bosnia would never celebrate July 11 as Srebrenica Victims Memorial Day, or March 1 as the Day of Independence, or November 25 as the Day of Statehood. Practically, there was an agreement on January 1 as New Year's Day, May 1 as Labor Day, and May 9 as the Day of Victory over Nazism—but these are all holidays taken from other European countries. The Serbian speakers insisted that the Dayton Agreements Day, which produced peace in Bosnia-Herzegovina, should be celebrated as the national day of statehood. Because the high representative is not going to impose this law, we will not get it for a long time. This discussion revealed our conflicting views on what kind of nation Bosnia-Herzegovina is and on what kind of state we all need.

Catholic Identity and Aspects of the Common Good in Bosnia-Herzegovina

Priests and religious ministers are looked on as the friends of simple people, because in our region, while empires have emerged, stayed for a couple of centuries or decades, and then fallen, and states and governments have risen and disappeared, the populations of different religious and ethnic identities have remained. This is why we who preside at weekly services of worship can educate our respective congregations for peaceful living and for the constructive building of a civil society, fully aware that we cannot and should not take the place of political representatives and civil authorities.

In my experience of forty years' priestly service to Catholic communities in Travnik, Zenica, and Sarajevo, I feel that my fellow Catholics expect from their priests support in their ethnicity as well as in their religious beliefs. I know that some well-intentioned foreign Catholics point to such religiosity as being ethnic or nationalistic, but it is the only way in which we can serve concrete individuals and congregations in their life situations. In the view of any believer, religion is indeed an important element of people's identity, but it is not the only one.

It is well known that the Holy See defended the right of small nations to self-determination, in the process of the disintegration of the Soviet Union, Yugoslavia, and Czechoslovakia. In the case of Bosnia-Herzegovina, Pope John Paul II, in his numerous statements during the recent war, expressed his conviction that Bosnia-Herzegovina is viable as one state with three ethnic communities but should be assisted by the international community and respected by neighboring countries. This was the gist of his speeches and homilies made during his pastoral visit to Sarajevo in April 1997 and to Banja Luka on June 22, 2003. Therefore Catholic leaders would like all Catholics to remain in the country and to share with citizens of other religious and ethnic identities in common needs, rights, duties, and tasks. It is possible to reconcile one's Catholic belief, Croat ethnicity, and Bosnian citizenship by building the bridges of forgiveness and trust. Pope John Paul II, in his address to our collective presidency on April 13, 1997, stated:

> Building a true and lasting peace is a great task entrusted to everyone. Certainly, much depends on those who have public responsibilities. But the future of peace, while largely entrusted to institutional formulations, which have to be effectively drawn up by means of sincere dialogue and respect for justice, depends no less decisively on a renewed solidarity of minds and hearts. It is this interior attitude which must be fostered, both within the frontiers of Bosnia-Herzegovina and also in relations with neighbouring states and the community of nations. But an attitude of this kind can only be established on a foundation of forgiveness. For the edifice

of peace to be solid, against the background of so much blood and hatred, it will have to be built on the courage of forgiveness. People must know how to ask for forgiveness and how to forgive![35]

Our Catholic faith enables us to cherish Catholic identity living among fellow citizens of other religious and ethnic identities. The same faith asks us to go on living as individuals and as a community in the country where we have been born and raised because we see it as God's will for us. Aware as we are of the conflicting evaluations of distant and of recent history in this country, we know that it is not a simple matter to identify the elements of the common good where we can contribute together with fellow citizens of other religious, ethnic, and cultural identities. In the current situation, we all agree that integration into the European Union would enable us to respect each other's rights and needs and to build up a pluralistic civil society.

The *Catechism of the Catholic Church* deals with the common good in its chapter on "Participation in Social Life," within the section on the moral life of baptized believers.[36] It draws the task of contributing toward the common good from the social nature of the human person, because the permanent good of each person is "necessarily related to the common good. . . . By the common good is to be understood the sum total of social conditions which allow people, either as groups or as individuals, to reach their fulfilment more fully and more easily."[37] Accordingly, the *Catechism* calls for prudence from ordinary citizens and civil authorities at three levels: respect for the person as such, the social well-being and development of the group, and peace as "the stability and security of a just order." It is in the political community that the most complete realization of the common good can be achieved.[38]

In my involvement in interreligious dialogue in Bosnia-Herzegovina for the sake of the common good, I use several books written by American Catholic scholars, as they sustain reflections along the guidelines of the Catholic magisterium and their Christian experience within a pluralistic society.[39] One of these writers, David Hollenbach, points out that civil society is constituted by a host of diverse social, economic, political, and cultural interactions: "Each of these relationships is capable of realizing some aspect of the human good. The historical, earthly common good, therefore, is an ensemble of diverse goods. These include goods achieved in family relationships, in voluntary associations, in political activity, in economic life, in the church, etc. It is important to note that this ensemble of goods is not cleanly divisible into the political good on the one hand and a large set of 'private goods' on the other."[40] I find very helpful Hollenbach's concept of "intellectual solidarity" as shared vision and the building up of a pluralistic civil society. This is what we believers and the other citizens of Bosnia-Herzegovina need.

In conclusion, I draw attention to the complexities of the approach to nationhood and loyalty to one's homeland in Bosnia-Herzegovina, as this depends on our ethnic and religious identities. Christianity and Islam are universal religions, existing in many nations and in diverse cultures. As believing citizens of this country, we should rely on our faith in contributing toward the common good in our pluralistic society.

The Identity of Christians in Church and in State

Bogdan Lubardič

Identity in Church

To "be" (*einai*) means to find, or to keep trying to find, a human answer to the mystery of being. To be a Christian means that this answer is found, or ever *re*-appropriated, with Christ in God.[41] For a Christian, then, living in Christ is truly being a human being—humanity being meaningfully transformed on its way to God (*ho ōn*).[42] The way of existence of this life in Christ is the horizon that discloses our identity, because identity—in the ontological sense[43]—means to constitute a (true) *way* of being (*tropos hyparxeōs*), and Christ discloses to us that we cannot truly be (1 John 5:12)—that we cannot have true identity[44]—if we do not live as Church, that is, as a liturgical community sharing the Eucharistic sacrament of Love.[45] This sacrament is given to us in the concrete life-giving body and blood of Christ, the Son of God.[46] Communio(n) in and with Christ means to receive our identity as the way of love, and, indeed, "abide in my love (*agapē*)," says the Lord (John 15:9; 1 John 1:7). This love is not just discourse "about" love but Love Himself (*ho Theos*).[47] Hence it is indissolubly intertwined with personal sacrifice offered for the life of the world and everyone in the world.[48] To be thence means to be as (*homoios*) Christ: to live in Christ and with Christ *as* he does with the Father in the Spirit. In other words, this is to draw existence from a community of love for the other (*allos*) and for everything other— even at the price of traversing across complete self-denial (*kenosis*) unto death itself. This community is realized in the Eucharist as Church and, by the same token, as the historic way that God lives with us extending the blessing of meaningful being to humanity.[49] However, this is possible only to the extent that we freely accept to be (to have identity) through the reciprocal sacrifice of love in the liturgic, Eucharistic way of being—to be, in St. Paul's words, "in the *cross* of our Lord Jesus Christ" (Gal. 6:14). This means not only to live out or to simulate the sacrifice of love (as "culture" of cult, or even as "ritualism") but also to love sacrifice and to battle for it—really to bleed for the other (John 19:34). In other words, to have identity in Christ means to sacrifice oneself in order to share love with the other and, more importantly, for the other.[50] And there is the whole world to sacrifice—my whole "self"[51] and all of its "pride of life" (1 John 2:16): biological, sociopolitical, economic, class, status, ethno-national, and, most paradoxically, religious and even confessional pride.[52] That is, one can die for someone [other] despite their religious identity or belief: for example, Mother Maria Skobtsova.[53] For sacrifice is sacrifice if and only if love covers and transcends everything.[54] Nothing less is what the liturgy of Church—as the life of God in man and vice versa—makes real and existent, thus showing itself to be the transforming telos of created being. It is this, in its core, that the Apostle Paul calls the "celestial policy" (*to politeuma en ouranois*) of the faithful church (Philem. 3:20). The apostolic tradition of the fathers of the Orthodox Church nurtures this kind of understanding of ecclesial identity, that is, the identity of the church. For instance, St. Symeon the New Theologian, speaking of St. Paul's ineffable experience of the goods prepared by God for those who love Him (1 Cor. 2:9), states that "*together* with the good things stored up in heaven, these are the Body and Blood of our Lord Jesus Christ which we see every day and eat and drink. . . . Outside of these, you will *not* be able to find one of those things spoken of, even if you . . . traverse the whole creation."[55] Likewise, for St. Nicolas Cabasilas, the liturgy as Eucharistic way of life *is* the foretaste of the Kingdom of God: it is always already the living Christ *hic et nunc.*[56]

The Christian does have a "political" identity, but this is simultaneously and primarily liturgical, and this, further still, means that to live the liturgical sacrifice of love is to battle historically, sociopolitical influence notwithstanding, for created being (*ktisis*) as the beginning of "things coming to be" in and for communion with God (*en koinōnia gignesthai*).[57]

Identity in State

Because the church is God living with humanity, it may be said that the church in principle is never outside the Divine–human context, that is, she is never totally outside history or metahistory. This context may be taken to mean all the things that God wishes for humanity and all the things that God allows ("tolerates") humans to experience, understand, and build, even those that are not explicitly according to His will. It is probably safe to say that the reality of the state is a structure in the realm of being that is offered or allowed to humans to create in order to manifest, organize, and develop the potentialities of human nature. It can be defined as a system of institutions catering for human needs or rights, both as individual and as collective. However, there is but one need of concrete and personal humanity that the state cannot meet, satisfy, and fulfill: the need for life beyond and despite death. Furthermore, neither can this "need" or, better still, this right to the holiness of eternal life be fulfilled by the instance of the nation as a system of symbols or institutions designed to produce "identity" through a common experience of language, culture, ethnic sameness, and geo-history and thus to cater for another set of human needs or "rights."[58] Because it is God who is Life itself, it is clear that outside God as Church, there cannot be victory over death, nor can the state or nation take the place of God or Church in that respect (John 5:26). Sadly enough, they often do. The basic difference, then, between state and nation vis-à-vis God as Church is that only in Church may we consummate and realize our right to eternal and holy life (*theōsis*). The method, or ecclesial "politic," is indicated by Christ and is identical to His way of sacrificial being: "give blood and receive spirit (i.e., life)," as the fathers of the Church teach.[59] Viewed from this perspective, it seems that human identity constituted by the state, nation, or civic society—as particular ways of being oneself with others[60]—is a necessary but by no means sufficient condition for meaningful existence, as these instances cannot meet death and overcome it, as does the Lord Jesus Christ, as the "pillar and bulwark" of true Life (1 Tim. 3:15).

 The liturgical identity of a Christian is specifically different from his identity as member of a state or a nation. The main reason is that the state or nation cannot truly heal, sanctify, and save him from death (although they may protect him from injury or ignorance). However, it is precisely for this reason that the church accepts both the state and the nation, but in order to act on both instances in Christ (*en Christō*)—that is, by showing the way of divine transformation of human nature in sacrificial and Eucharistic love. Hence, although ever differing from them, the church "dies" for them too, leading the way to God in Christ.

Challenge of Mediation: The Serbian Orthodox Church and the Tradition of St. Sava .

The Orthodox Church of Christ accepted by the Serbs living in the Balkans, Bosnia notwithstanding, has a decisive and most formative imprint given to it in the person of St. Sava Nemanjić (1175–1236). More precisely, this imprint is given by the twofold historic event of the Žiča Synod of Serb people in 1221,[61] where St. Sava *liturgically* "presided" over the crowning of the first prince Stephan (St. Symeon, d. 1228)[62] and the declaration of the *Synodikon of Orthodoxy*,[63] the all-foundational set of Christian canon laws binding for both members of the church (believers) and members of the Serbian state (citizens). In both events the hallmark of the Serbian Orthodox Christian tradition, known popularly as *svetosavlje*, was made particularly apparent and meaningful for centuries to come until the present day. In what sense? First, the event of coronation was taken to mean that the prince has become similar to the bishop, in dispassion (*apatheia*).[64] Namely, he already has stately power but not as yet holiness; hence the church, personified in the name of St. Sava, confirms by an action of grace that he has accomplished the preconditions leading to holiness: humility and sacrificial love for the other. Thus is set the ideal for the secular order (later exemplified by the institution of state and ruler, not necessarily in the form of a kingdom).[65] Second, the event of declaring the *Synodikon*, solemnly accepted by both the bishop and the prince-ruler, makes known the pledge of the Serbian people to follow the Christian tradition in the Orthodox key and by the same token to take both ecclesial and state responsibility for preserving the purity of the Christian way of existence.

Thus is set the ideal for relations between church and state or nation, for churchhood and statehood identity, respectively. The figures of ruler and bishop symbolize the state and the church. They meet in a relation of symphonic accord, mutually bettering each other: the bishop (as icon of Christ) by making it possible for every person to unite and identify with God in Christ by means of grace, escaping death in the church; the ruler by protecting the institutions and laws of state, for thus are protected the very citizens ("subjects") whose final goal is to attain a par excellence ecclesial identity.[66] Hence are avoided the trappings both of *papocesarism*, where the church rules instead of the state, and of *cesaropapism*, where it is the other way around.[67] Moreover, St. Sava first and foremost preaches the acceptance of Christ and the Church, not of an étatist or nationalist ideology.[68] He proves this by renouncing everything (both as ex-prince and as monk) except Christ. In that sense, *svetosavlje* as the historic way of Serbian Christianity is, or must again become, nonnationalist and simultaneously patriotic in the Pauline sense of "celestial" or liturgical "politics."

Today the same must hold true for the Serbian Orthodox Church and its relation toward the state and the nation, particularly in a multireligious and multinational and, more and more so, a transnational ("global") context and perspective. One cannot claim without due reserve that there is or should be a substantial identity between state and ethnic nation on one hand and church on the other, unless it is to do grievous harm to both. Rather, as authentic *svetosavlje* also witnesses, the two relate in mutual cooperation and simultaneous differentiation:[69] state and nation protect and enrich each individual (as the concrete common "good"), and the church sanctifies and saves everyone as person (as the prime Gospel good). This also means that in the state and nation there is room for many, and these may be the other(s)—our other(s): because we form our deepest identity in God's all-inclusive love, not (only) in structures that cannot or that refuse to constitute their identity in a reserveless sacrifice for the other (*alter*-nativus).

Liturgical identity is always a "political" identity in St. Paul's sense, but not every political identity is necessarily liturgical (although, in principle, it does come under its influence). That is why it is extremely dangerous to identify the two types or levels of identity, when the state, nation, or even "civil society" become "god." More important, that is why the later identity should be mediated with the former, ecclesial identity, by merit of which both state and nation recognize their ontological and historical limits, thus becoming open for the salvific action of God in Christ, but not necessarily becoming reduced, assimilated, or destroyed (as in exclusive fundamentalism).

It seems that this is the message that the Serbian Orthodox Church wishes to reinstate in European Bosnia and the European Balkans: both as an unavoidable self-critique (of perhaps failing always to distinguish vigorously and to prevent true faith from being manipulated along lines of politicized "religious recourses")[70] and as an instigation for (our) others to keep reexamining their own positions of religious-cultural and sociopolitical behavior. This presupposes that Europe accepts responsibility for hearing the voices (screams, in fact) of Bosnian-Balkan Europe.[71] Because these are its own (complementary and internal, not necessarily external) voices, rising from within the "muted" but inerasable Balkan (br)other(s), the Balkans present "Europe" with a horizon for painful but cathartic further self-understanding. For it is in Bosnia, as a sui generis Balkan Jerusalem, that concrete people have been meeting death from under the rubble of nationalist, étatist, and religious ideology, not without feedback from a neoimperial Balkanistic power discourse and political practice.[72] If this deconstructive imperative fails to be met by all of us together, the words of Slavoj Žižek, warning that "the Balkans always remain the [*alien*] other,"[73] will persist, echoing in Maria Todorova's critical statement:

> By being geographically inextricable from Europe, yet culturally constructed as an "other" within, the Balkans have been able to absorb conveniently a number of externalised political, ideological, and cultural frustrations stemming from tensions and contradictions inherent to the regions and societies outside the Balkans. Balkanism became, in time, a convenient substitute for the emotional discharge that orientalism provided, exempting the West from charges of racism, colonialism, Eurocentrism, and Christian intolerance against Islam. After all, the Balkans are in Europe; they are white; they are predominantly Christian, and therefore the externalisation of frustrations on them can circumvent the usual racial or religious bias allegations.[74]

Excursus: On Dying for an Other

Confessionalism grounds Christian identity in propositional intellectualizations of faith. Confessional identity remains in stark contrast to primordial Christian identity, which is primarily drawn from conforming to God through the way of existence of Christ, that is, unconditional kenotic sacrifice manifested in the Eucharistic community of the faithful. It is the Spirit who introduces (*introitium*) or offers (*sacrificium*) Christ to all of creation both "cat-holically" and "trans-confessionally," without necessarily diluting the Eucharistic-ecclesial anchoring point of divine action (1 Cor. 12:3). In fact, it is the Father Himself who sends out the Spirit (*parakletos*) in the name of Christ, fulfilling the salvific *oikonomia* (John 14:25–26). Hence God may be found outside the Eucharistic-ecclesial community *stricto sensu*, for the Spirit transcends even the instance of ecclesial sameness of the already faithful. This is made possible by the spiritual operation of divine Charity, which wills to be universal (*cat-holic*) and open to all. Therefore God's love is ideally manifested in the Eucharist, but not exclusively, for the Spirit simultaneously reaches out to others and everything other. Lamentably, confessionalism fails to see that God is not reducible to formal "symbols of faith" as conditions for faith or "reasons" for love. For the Spirit, ever preconfessionally, beckons all of creation to participate in the Father's love through the all-inclusive and open sacrifice of Christ. Thus, even before baptism, not to mention "in-confessionalization," the unboundable and unrestrainable Spirit views every individual in terms of his or her potentially sacramental, Eucharistic-ecclesial identity: as sons and daughters to be (Gen. 1:1; John 3:8). The economy of the Spirit excludes conditioning the love of Christ by confessional "credentials," for it is realized as pure charity: not only as transconfessional but even as "transreligious." Apologetic "missionarism," as the practical fuel of confessionalism, is not the reason why one might or should die for the other. The principal reason for "dying" for any other—Jew, Christian, Muslim, Buddhist, or whomever—is that of living as Christ in Christ for no other reason whatsoever but re-presencing divine love in its own, albeit ecclesial, worth. Dying for a foreigner in faith, or for someone foreign to faith, or for someone of a foreign faith, is thus the ultimate test of sacrificial likening (*homoiōsis*) to God. Finally, is not God Himself our Other too?

Faith and National Identity in Britain

Zaki Badawi and Michael Ipgrave

The subject of citizenship is a recent addition to the United Kingdom national school curriculum, introduced as a way of instructing young people in the rights and responsibilities of participation in British society. Recent too has been the devising of "citizenship ceremonies" at which those wishing to become British citizens publicly declare their intention of doing so and have their new status officially acknowledged. Both of these developments are evidence of a growing and self-conscious concern on the part of the British state to articulate the meaning of "citizenship." This kind of attempt to define citizenship is a new phenomenon. Historically, insofar as status as a British citizen could be said to have legally definable content, this was derived from the allegiance owed by a subject to the sovereign and thus could be expressed in terms of his or her subjection to the laws of the realm. To that extent, citizenship of the United Kingdom has historically been a concept formally devoid of any particular ethnic, cultural, or religious associations other than those that were implied by being a loyal subject of the Crown.

Paradoxically this archaic and minimalist conception of citizenship as allegiance has, through its very lack of definition, helped to facilitate a diversity of ethnic, cultural, and religious paths of British citizenship, Christian and Muslim paths among them. In what follows we point to three important features of the historical processes that have allowed this to happen before turning to some more contemporary reflections on Muslim and Christian identities in relation to British citizenship.

49

Three Features from History

The first simple, but critically important, point to note about the history that has formed the idea of British citizenship is that it embraces not one national story but several. Leaving aside for now the passionately contested, and at times tortured, struggles over identity and citizenship that mark the island of Ireland, on the other island of Great Britain there are three distinct but intertwined histories of England, Scotland, and Wales, not to mention the further complexities that emerge when regional and local substories are taken into account. The distinctions between the three have been perhaps most apparent in terms of religious history, and all currently differ in their patterns of church–state relations. In England, Anglican Christianity has that measure of official control, privilege, and responsibility that is encompassed in the status of an established church. In Scotland, a rather different set of arrangements provide for the recognition of Presbyterian Christianity as a national church. In Wales, no form of Christianity has any more official standing than another. All three British nations are further characterized by significant religious pluralities, both among Christians and more widely among people of different faiths.

This geographical pluriformity has resulted, as a by-product, in the availability of two levels of language for assigning identity in national terms. Thus people can describe themselves as "English," "Scottish," or "Welsh," or they can describe themselves as "British." These two ways of speaking are not simply related as specific and generic denotations. They can carry quite different emotional and relational connotations—a point that often seems more apparent to Scottish and Welsh than to many English people. "English" is of all the descriptors the one that comes closest to having a specific ethnic content: Whereas it is common, for example, to speak of "Black British," the phrase "Black English" is very unusual and indeed sounds rather odd.[75] Conversely, and positively, it can be argued that the existence of more than one dimension of national identity has been helpful in facilitating a plurality of ways of citizenship.

Second, the idea of a citizenship that can be shared by people of different religions has grown in a gradual and piecemeal way in the British context. There has until recently been no clearly articulated statement of the rights and responsibilities of citizenship realized at any definite point of time. In England the story has been that of a transition from the idea of a comprehensive national church coterminous in its membership with the secular body politic, through a more or less grudging acknowledgment and toleration of the presence of non-Anglicans, to the successive removal of all impediments to their citizenship. The bars to citizenship for those outside the Church of England were removed in different stages: freedom of worship was generally the first to be granted, then further steps such as the registration of corporately held property, permission to hold certain public offices, the recognition of marriages, and so eventually to acceptance of full participation in civic life. Different groups such as Protestant dissenters, Quakers, Jews, Roman Catholics, and atheists proceeded through these processes at different rates in English history, as from the late seventeenth to the mid-nineteenth centuries various pieces of permissive legislation were enacted, or restrictive legislation was repealed.[76]

This pragmatic and untidy process has meant that the British context of citizenship incorporates, as it were, a prehistory of that religious pluralism that has developed as a result of large-scale immigration in the later twentieth century. Before the advent in Britain of significant Muslim, Hindu Sikh, and other religious communities, the development of intra-Christian diversity, and the negotiation of that diversity in terms of social policy, had resulted in a looser texture to public life that helped to make possible the subsequent acceptance of other faith groups in society. Moreover, if the attitudes in the latter process have at times been tense or even hostile, it should be remembered that in preecumenical times relations between different Christian traditions in British history were also at times very difficult. The simplistic picture of a homogeneous Christian society whose harmony was suddenly challenged by the arrival of swarms of non-Christian immigrants fails entirely to acknowledge the bitterness of intra-Christian divisions, from the martyrs on every side of the Reformation era to the struggles over church schools between Anglicans, Roman Catholics, and Protestant nonconformists in the late nineteenth centuries. It also has to be recognized that that bitterness was often in the past inflamed by the determination of some members of the established church to cling to their privileged positions.

Third, although the previous description has been couched in religious terms, and this in general reflects the language of the debates over citizenship as they arose in the course of history, the principal cause for the exclusion of religious minorities in British history seems to have been neither theological nor spiritual. For example, however convinced Protestant Anglicans may have been of the falsity of some Roman Catholic doctrines, the exclusion of Roman Catholics from civic life was not on the basis of any principle that "error has no rights" but rather out of a concern over the political allegiance of those whose faith required of them an obedience to the pope in Rome.[77] Again, a significant extant piece of English legislation reflecting a "Christendom mentality," the common law provision on blasphemy, although now seen as providing protection for people's religious feelings, has its origins in an age when an attack on the established religion was tantamount to an attack on royal authority itself.[78]

Thus there has historically been a strong political factor in British hostility to the civic inclusion of people of different religious identities. In the case of anti–Roman Catholic sentiment in England, this has been linked to anxiety about obedience to a foreign authority and the fears that this could result, at best, in divided loyalties and, at worst, in disloyalty to the nation. The prevalence of this political-national concern over religious-theological considerations is dramatically shown by the dramatic turnabout in attitudes toward Roman Catholics in the course of a few years at the end of the eighteenth century. In 1780, the Gordon Riots saw a violent frenzy of "anti-Papist" hysteria in London, but only a decade later émigré monastic communities from France were warmly welcomed in England, not least because they were perceived as hostile to the French revolutionary regime with whom Britain was by that stage at war. To the degree that this strand of insularist thinking persists in the United Kingdom today, it is natural to wonder how far fears of "double allegiance" have contributed to suspicion of, or hostility toward, Muslims in British society.

Bearing in mind the shaping influence on contemporary attitudes of these historical factors, what can we say about Islamic and Christian religious identities in relation to British citizenship today?

Muslims and British Citizenship

Muslims in Britain are living in a society neither governed by Muslims nor regulated according to the principles of Islam; their presence in that country is largely a consequence of the freely taken decision of many Muslims to come to live there.[79] This raises the following questions: Should Muslims choose to live in a non-Muslim context in this way? If they do choose so to do, what should be their attitude to participation in its civil life?

The situation of Muslims under non-Islamic governance is one that has arisen previously in Islamic history. Following the end of Muslim power in Spain, for example, the communities there sought guidance from scholars in Morocco and in Egypt as to what their course of action should be and received a variety of responses. Those who counseled that emigration to a Muslim country was necessary pointed to Qur'anic verses such as the following, reproving those early members of the Muslim community who preferred to stay in Mecca, in a polytheistic environment with all the dangers to their practice of Islam which that involved, rather than to join in the hijra to Medina:

> When the angels take the souls of those who have wronged themselves, they ask them, "What circumstances were you in?" They reply, "We were oppressed in this land," and the angels say, "But was God's earth not spacious enough for you to migrate to some other place?" These people will have Hell as their refuge, an evil destination.[80]

> Say [Prophet], "If your fathers, sons, brothers, wives, tribes, the wealth you have acquired, the trade which you fear will decline, and the dwellings you love are dearer to you than God and His Messenger and the struggle in his cause, then wait until God brings about his punishment." God does not guide those who break away. (al-Tawba 9:24; cf. also al-Nisā' 4:144)

They also pointed to a hadith (oral tradition with regard to Mohammad) that enjoins the maintenance of a clear distance between Muslims and non-Muslims:

> "I am not responsible for any Muslim who stays among polytheists." They said, "Why, Apostle of Allah?" He said: "Their fires should not be visible to one another."[81]

Conversely, those who advised the Muslims to remain where they were, and to participate as fully as Islamically possible in non-Muslim society, pointed to a well-known hadith that declared the cessation of the requirement to emigrate: "There is no more hijra after the conquest of Mecca."[82]

Lying behind these different opinions are different attitudes toward the status of non-Muslim governments, and so to the extent to which Muslims can faithfully live in non-Muslim countries. A rigorist view categorically divides the world into the two realms of *dār al-islām* and *dār al-ḥarb*, respectively, the "House of Islam" and the "House of War." The former embraces those countries subject to Islamic law and the latter, all other places. The duty of every Muslim living in the latter is, in this way of thinking, either to fight for its transformation into, or to emigrate to, the former. If conditions for this are for the moment unpropitious, in any case, Muslims in their present situation should have no participation in the civil or political life of the *dār al-ḥarb*. It must be noted that such an ideology—revived in our own days by separationist groups calling for Muslims to withdraw from British society—cannot simply be read from the pages of the Qur'ān but instead relies on a particular interpretation of scriptural verses and the tradition. Interpretation, however, is always contingent to some extent on the situation of the interpreter, and it can be clearly seen that there are several factors that point to the need for a different reading of Islamic duties to meet the situation of Muslim communities in Britain.

Broadly speaking, Muslim communities are found in Britain because Muslims have chosen to live there, they continue to live there because it is in their best interests to stay there, and it is quite possible for them to fulfill their duties as faithful Muslims while living there. In such circumstances, it could even be argued that a society such as Britain should be counted as part of the *dār al-islām*, in that it is a place where the practice of Islam is freely allowed to Muslims—in some senses with fewer restrictions than in some Muslim countries.[83] In any case, it is certain that the rigorist division of the world into two clear-cut and mutually opposed camps does not at all answer the situation of Muslim communities in Britain and cannot be invoked to justify either the necessity of emigration or withdrawal from civic life.

In light of this, several scholars recently have looked with fresh interest at a third category recognized in Islamic tradition as lying between *dār al-islām* and *dār al-ḥarb*—namely, the so-called *dār al-sulh*, or *dār al-ahd*, the "House of Treaty": domains where the position of Muslims is guaranteed by some form of compact (historically, a treaty with a nearby Muslim state).[84] Whatever traditional framework of interpretation is used or adapted to meet the current situation, though, it is apparent that Muslims living within the freedoms guaranteed by British society have the ability, indeed the obligation, to participate fully in the rights and responsibilities conveyed by British citizenship.

Of course, for such a sense of citizenship to be nurtured and fully appropriated among British Muslims, it is necessary that their self-perception should be such as to make them feel comfortable in the British context. There are factors that militate to some degree against this: There is unquestionably an anti-Islamic bias in some parts of the media. Racism and xenophobia in some parts of society persist and can be particularly directed against Muslim communities. Perhaps most difficult of all, the repeated and suspicious interrogation of Muslims as to their primary loyalty is profoundly unhelpful. Like Christianity, Islam is a universal religion; to ask people to place in a hierarchy alternative descriptions such as "British Muslim" or "Muslim living in Britain" is completely to fail to acknowledge the universal sense of belonging that Muslims will naturally feel. Most of all, like a Christian or a person of any other faith or of none, a Muslim will know that his or her primary and overarching loyalty is to the human race. Within that allegiance, understood by Muslims in terms of the solidarity of shared creaturehood and stewardship, the duty of citizenship lays a positive obligation on Muslims to participate as citizens in the life of the societies in which they live, provided those societies respect their fundamental religious freedoms and do not gratuitously alienate them. In the British context, that means in particular that Muslims have a duty to enter the political process, as voters, candidates, and officeholders. One of the encouraging signs of the growing recognition of citizenship as a responsibility for Muslims in Britain is the extent to which this political engagement was realized in the 2005 United Kingdom general election.

Christians and British Citizenship

The concept of "citizenship," insofar as it can be identified within British history, was originally centered in the public practice of one form of Christianity, whether Anglican or Presbyterian. While the extension of citizenship took place through the removal of disabilities from those not so practicing, this has been accompanied by no weakening of the sense that Anglican or Presbyterian Christians are in the fullest sense citizens in England or Scotland, respectively. Changes in both society and the churches, though, have now resulted in a considerable range of Christian attitudes to the relationship between faith and citizenship in Britain. Among the changes in society must be mentioned the often discussed, but still elusive, set of phenomena known as "secularization," the growth of other faith communities and of nonreligious ways of thinking and the development of human rights thinking that emphasizes the need for equal recognition to be accorded to all religious groups. Within the churches there have been major changes also: the ethnic and cultural diversification of British Christianity as a result of immigration; the formation of a bewildering variety of new churches; the sense of ecumenical rapprochement that has grown up among the historic churches; and the strengthening within the British churches of solidarity with Christians overseas, particularly with those living as minorities in difficult situations. As a result, while an overwhelming consensus of Christian thought in Britain clearly accepts the privileges and obligations of citizenship and teaches the importance of responsible engagement by the churches within civil society, within this consensus there are very significant differences of emphasis, particularly over the extent to which and the way in which religious faith should be acknowledged, affirmed, or even protected by society.[85]

As an example of this, it is helpful to consider the varied responses made by British Christians to repeated government proposals to introduce new legislation to outlaw incitement to religious hatred. The legal background is as follows. The common law provision of blasphemy at present gives some measure of protection from offensive attack to the Christian religion, at least in the form in which it is professed by the established Church of England, although in practice the law has not been successfully used since 1979 (during which time the Church of England has scarcely been immune from attack).[86] Adherents of other faiths are as such afforded no protection for their religious beliefs, though those faith communities that approximate to ethnic groups are covered by race relations legislation.[87] Acting from a particular concern over the vulnerability of British Muslims to attack on the grounds of their faith, the British government has repeatedly sought to introduce new legislation to curb activities that stir up hatred against people on the grounds of their religion or belief, though at the time of this writing no law has successfully completed its passage through Parliament. These proposals have elicited very different responses from churches and Christian organizations and can in a sense be seen as a litmus revealing a variety of attitudes to citizenship in contemporary Britain. Three broad positions can be distinguished.

First, some groups have argued strenuously against the provision of any form of protection to other religious groups, while insisting that the blasphemy law should remain in place to safeguard Christianity.[88] The dual arguments advanced for such a position are, first, that Christianity is the true religion and therefore deserving of protection in a way that other, "false" religions are not, and second, that the United Kingdom is in its constitution and history a Christian nation. The advancement of true Christianity in this view could well require the strident denigration of other religions, and such denigration would be inhibited by new legislation in this area. In its unabashed request for a dramatically preferential position for Christianity to be maintained by the civic authorities, this view represents a harking back to a Christendom mentality that can find no place in the plural situation of contemporary Britain, not least because its logic seems by extension to imply that the full privileges of citizenship should be restricted to only Christians.

A second position, which is strongly held among many evangelicals in particular, does not seek a privileged position for Christian faith from the civic authorities but does vigorously oppose the introduction of a new law on the grounds that this would impede the church's primary task of evangelism.[89] Proponents of this view claim that if legislation were put in place, however carefully the provisions were drafted, there would be the inevitable consequence that those criticizing other religions as false, unethical, or deficient in any way would find themselves subject to legal challenge. So important is the task of proclaiming Christian truth, in this view, that it should override any concerns over social harmony or the vulnerability of other groups. A further argument sometimes advanced is that healthy inter faith relations in fact rely on the possibility of robust criticism of one another by those assenting to competing truth claims. It is interesting to note that Christians employing this approach find themselves in alliance with secular libertarian advocates of free speech with whom they theologically have nothing in common. Both hold that a sense of citizenship is best nurtured in the religious dimension by an unconstrainedly free market of ideas.

Third, the position of the historic churches has been generally much more positive toward the idea of new legislation.[90] This, it is argued, would be designed to protect religious believers as individuals and communities rather than the beliefs they hold; it would distinguish between robust criticism (which would continue to be legal) and the instigation of hatred (which would not); and it should pose no problem for Christian evangelism, which as the proclamation of good news surely should not rely on the promotion of hatred for its success. Positively, those in favor of a new law insist that it is needed for the protection of vulnerable groups, to remedy perceived inequities in existing provisions and to delineate a safe arena within which positive inter faith relations can be built up with confidence. It can be seen that this approach lays great emphasis on the task of building a shared sense of citizenship across different religious communities, showing a concern to guarantee legally the conditions that will allow such sharing in much the same way as race relations legislation was designed to achieve the same goal in the multiethnic dimension.

Lying behind these three different responses to a particular legislative proposal are three rather different attitudes to the relation of citizenship and faith and to the way in which Christians should engage with other faith communities in the public sphere.[91] In the first view, citizenship has a status derivative from, and subordinate to, Christian faith, and any civic space for people of other faiths can only be grudgingly admitted within this Christendom paradigm. In the second view, citizenship is primarily a way of providing a context within which Christian faith can be freely manifested and propagated. It is recognized that this context should equally be open to other faith expressions also, but religious commitment must always be accorded primacy over civic involvement. In the third view, citizenship and Christian faith are placed in a constructive relationship with one another, and other faiths too are accorded a place within the civic project. Indeed, in this view, one of the roles of the state is to make provision for the full participation of all religious groups in civic life, so as to enable their contribution to the common good.

It seems certain that the first of these three options is unsustainable in the plural society of the contemporary United Kingdom, and the future of British Christianity lies with either the second or the third option. Whatever the long-term outcome may be, it is evident that profound theological questions are at issue here. Christians can and must be as deeply exercised as their Muslim fellow citizens over what it means to live as faithful believers and responsible citizens in contemporary Britain.

Notes

1. Rainer Maria Rilke, "The Ninth Elegy" from "The Duino Elegies," in *Selected Poems*, trans. J. B. Leishman (London: Penguin, 1964).

2. I would like to thank the participants at the Building Bridges seminar May 15–20, 2005, in Sarajevo, Bosnia, for their invaluable assistance with this project. I would also like to thank the organizers of the *Guardian* seminar on "Islam, Race and Identity" in January 2005 for providing a forum for discussions and all the participants for their thoughtful comments.

3. Michael Oakeshott, "Rationalism in Politics," in *Rationalism in Politics* (London: Methuen, 1962), 1.

4. Ibid., 32.

5. Charles Taylor, *Sources of the Self: The Making of Modern Identity* (Cambridge, MA: Harvard University Press, 1989).

6. See, e.g., Joseph Raz, "Duties of Well Being," in *Ethics in the Public Domain: Essays in the Morality of Law and Politics* (Oxford: Clarendon, 1994), 27; Charles Taylor, *Multiculturalism and the Politics of Recognition* (Princeton, NJ: Princeton University Press, 1992).

7. For a discussion of the untenability of Rawls's distinction between private and public reasons for action, see John Finnis, "Is Natural Law Theory Compatible with Limited Government?" in *Natural Law, Liberalism and Morality*, ed. Robert George (Oxford: Clarendon Press, 1996), 9.

8. Taylor, *Multiculturalism and the Politics of Recognition*, 25–27. The importance of "recognition" finds an analogy in Hume's idea of the importance of "sympathy," which is a "fellow feeling or other-regarding concern [which] . . . establishes the essential link between the individual and the community." See Gerald Postema, *Bentham and the Common Law Tradition* (Oxford: Clarendon Press, 1986).

9. Paul Ricoeur, *Oneself as Another*, trans. Kathleen Blamey (Chicago: University of Chicago Press, 1992).

10. Alasdair MacIntyre, *After Virtue: A Study in Moral Theory*, 2nd ed. (Notre Dame, IN: University of Notre Dame Press, 1984).

11. For a recent discussion of these issues, see Seumas Milne, "The Struggle Is No Longer against Religion, but within It," *Guardian*, December 16, 2004.

12. Clifford Geertz, *The Interpretation of Cultures* (London: Fontana Press, 1993), 110–15.

13. Ibid., 111.

14. See Aref Nayed's essay on this issue in chapter 3 in this volume.

15. Milne, "Struggle."

16. Polly Toynbee, "We Must Be Free to Criticise without Being Called Racist," *Guardian*, August 18, 2004.

17. "He is quick, thinking in clear images; I am slow, thinking in broken images. . . . When the facts fail him, he questions his senses; when the facts fail me, I approve my senses. He continues quick and dull in his clear images; I continue slow and sharp in my broken images. He in a new confusion of his understanding; I in a new understanding of my confusion." Robert Graves, "In Broken Images," *Selected Poems* (London: Penguin, 1986).

18. For a fuller discussion of ritual along these lines, see Geertz, *Interpretation of Cultures,* 110–15.

19. For a discussion of the modern problem of "articulacy," see Charles Taylor, *The Ethics of Authenticity* (Cambridge, MA: Harvard University Press, 1991).

20. This position is worked out, in a sustained way, in the book of Daniel, for example.

21. See further C. E. B. Cranfield, *The Gospel according to St. Mark* (Cambridge: Cambridge University Press, 1966), 371–72. Also see Alan Storkey, *Jesus and Politics: Confronting the Powers* (Grand Rapids, MI: Baker, 2005), 211ff.

22. See Colin Hemer, "The Letters to the Seven Churches of Asia in Their Local Setting," *Journal for the Study of the New Testament* 11 (1986): 7ff.

23. "City of God," 4:4, *Library of Nicene and Post-Nicene Fathers* (Edinburgh: T & T Clark, 1993), 66.

24. Storkey, *Jesus and Politics,* 184–85.

25. Lesslie Newbigin, *The Gospel in a Pluralist Society* (London: SPCK, 1989), 210.

26. See further Robert Sider, *The Gospel and Its Proclamation: Message of the Fathers of the Church* (Wilmington, DE: Michael Glazier, 1983).

27. William Young, *Patriarch, Shah and Caliph* (Rawalpindi: Christian Study Centre, 1974), 21–22.

28. See Jaroslav Pelikan, *The Excellent Empire: The Fall of Rome and the Triumph of the Church* (San Francisco, CA: Harper & Row, 1987); and George Every, *The Byzantine Patriarchate* (London: SPCK, 1947).

29. See further Owen Chadwick, *The Reformation* (London: Penguin, 1990).

30. Ibid., 14–15, 188ff.

31. See further Michael Nazir-Ali, "The Vocation of Anglicanism," *Anvil* 6, no. 2 (1989): 113ff, and *From Everywhere to Everywhere: A World View of Christian Mission* (London: HarperCollins, 1990), 46ff.

32. Rowan Williams and David Nicholls, *Politics and Theological Identity: Two Anglican Essays* (London: Jubilee, 1984), 21ff and 33ff.

33. In this debate, see George Weigel, *The Cube and the Cathedral: Europe, America and Politics without God* (New York: Basic Books, 2005).

34. "Epistle to Diognetus," 5.1–16, in *The Apostolic Fathers,* vol. 2, Kirsopp Lake, ed. and trans. (Cambridge, MA: Harvard University, Loeb Classical Library, 1913), 359–40. See also Michael Nazir-Ali, *Citizens and Exiles: Christian Faith in a Plural World* (London: SPCK, 1998).

35. Apostolic Visit of John Paul II to Sarajevo, *Address of the Holy Father to the Political Leaders of Bosnia-Hercegovina*, April 13, 1997, www.vatican .va/holy_father/john_paul_ii/travels (accessed June 5, 2008).

36. The *Catechism* was adopted by the magisterium in 1992 as the practical application of Vatican II for adult Catholics.

37. *Catechism*, §§ 1905–06.

38. Ibid., §§ 1907–12.

39. Among such writings are Vernon Ruland, *Conscience across Borders: An Ethics of Global Rights and Religious Pluralism* (San Francisco, CA: University of San Francisco Press, 2002); David Hollenbach, SJ, *The Common Good and Christian Ethics* (Cambridge: Cambridge University Press, 2002); and David Hollenbach, SJ, *The Global Face of Public Faith: Politics, Human Rights and Christian Ethics* (Washington, DC: Georgetown University Press, 2003).

40. Hollenbach, *Common Good*, 133.

41. J. D. Zizioulas, "The Theological Problem of 'Reception,'" *Bulletin* 26 (Centro pro Unione) (1984): 3–6.

42. For the locus classicus of an Orthodox understanding of biblical ontology as opposed to an essentialist Greek ontology, see St. Gregory Palamas's comment on Exodus 3.14 ("I am Who I am") in his *Third Triad in Defence of the Holy Hesychasts*, 2.12. (For the parallel locus in the Latin West, see St. Thomas Aquinas, *Summa Theologiae*, 1a 13, 11, where *qui est* is "the most appropriate name for God.")

43. In the Orthodox tradition, all types of identity are linkable to the ontological plane as they are never cut off from access to the divine grace of God (Eph. 2:18). Identity is not conceptualized exclusively in terms of

psychological, sociological, cultural, ethnic, or other typologies. More-over, the ontological is, or should be, projected into the listed types of identity. For example, many functions of Orthodox society have been grounded in the liturgy of the church, for example, marriage, the conse-cration of art, prayers for just rule, and so on.

44. Contemporary Orthodox theology is making successive attempts to "emancipate" the concept of identity from the Cartesian or Nietzschean understanding of identity constitution. Cf. Nicholas Loudovikos, "The Trinitarian Foundations and Anthropological Consequences of St Augustine's Spirituality and Byzantine 'Mysticism,'" *Philotheos* 1 (2001): 122–30.

45. The Orthodox theological stress on the *relational* (*schesis*) precondition for constituting authentic identity is acknowledged as a major contribu-tion to the contemporary debate on the subject–subjectivity problematic. One could, although somewhat awkwardly, speak of the "relational-communal a priori" of Orthodox *theoria* and *praxis* (borrowing the phrase from K.-O. Apel's transcendental language pragmatics, *Transfor-mation der Philosophie*, Frankfurt: Suhrkamp, 1972). P. McPartlan, *The Eucharist Makes the Church: H. de Lubac and J. Zizioulas in Dialogue* (Edinburgh: T & T Clark, 1992).

46. "I am the living bread (*ho artos ho zōn*) which came down from heaven; if any one eats of this bread, he will live for ever; and the bread which I shall give for the life of the world is my flesh . . . unless you eat the flesh (*tēn sarka*) of the Son of Man and drink his blood (*to haima*), you have no life in you." (John 6:47–58).

47. A. Schmemann, *The Eucharist* (Crestwood, NY: St. Vladimir's Seminary Press, 1987), 200–201.

48. Christ abides not (only) in obedience to an abstract and closed given of moral norm(s) but, preeminently, by loyalty and loving confidence to a *Person*—the Father (*ho Patēr*), thus personalizing any approach to mor-als. Cf. John 14:13, 15:10–11, 6:51. Also cf. A. Schmemann, *For the Life of the World: Sacraments and Orthodoxy* (Crestwood, NY: St Vladimir's Seminary Press, 1973), especially chap. 2.

49. J. D. Zizioulas, "The Ecclesiological Presuppositions of the Holy Eucha-rist," *Nicolaus* 10 (1982): 333–49.

50. This idea may be projected philosophically in terms of E. Levinas's *la substitution*, where a subject appears at the "place" of the other taking over not only his repentance but also his guilt—it opens a higher order

of "humanism." Cf. E. Levinas, *Otherwise Than Being or Beyond Essence* (Dordrecht: Kluwer, 1991) [Serbian: *Drugačije od bivstva ili s onu stranu bivstva* (Beograd: Nikšić, 1999)].

51. As St. John the Theologian explains: "the lust of the flesh and the lust of the eyes and the pride of life [*hē alazoneia tou biou*]" (1 John 2:16).

52. Christian faith is not a religion, as Christ *crosses* barriers from within (*ek tōn katō*: cf. St. Athanasius, *De Incarnatione*, 14), which is not the case in religion (which does not go *across* a living and incarnated God and His life-giving cross), even in view of its *re*-ligio. In fact, "religion" or "religiosity" may be indicators for gauging the reification of Christian faith and life.

53. See *Excursus* later, "On Dying for an Other." On Mother Maria Skobtsova (d. 1945), cf. N. Zernov, *The Russian Religious Renaissance of the XX Century* (New York: Harper & Row, 1963), 242–43. It would be most rewarding to investigate the Christian tradition in order to find occurrences and records of such sacrificial instances. I suggest exploring a "Historical Phenomenology of Sacrifice for the Wholly Other." It was Archbishop Rowan Williams who invoked the paradigmatic instance of Orthodox nun Maria Skobtsova. But others are waiting to be *re*-membered too.

54. "If I give away all I have . . . , but have not love, I gain *nothing*" (1 Cor. 13:3).

55. St. Symeon the New Theologian, *On the Mystical Life: The Ethical Discourses,* trans. A. Golitzin, vol. 1, "Third Ethical Discourse" (Crestwood, NY: St. Vladimir's Seminary Press, 1995), 130–31.

56. St. Nicholas Cabasilas, *Interpretation of the Divine Liturgy*, § 39 [Serbian, trans. S. Jakšić, *Tumačenje svete liturgije* (Novi Sad: Beseda, 2002), 143].

57. Further on the Maximian notion of "in-communion-becoming," cf. N. Loudovikos, *The Eucharistic Ontology* [in Greek] (Athens: Domos, 1992), and *An Apophatic Ecclesiology of Consubstantiality: Limits of Eucharistic Ecclesiology* [in Greek] (Athens: Armos, 2002), 68–93.

58. This "right" is a gift of divine grace (*charis*). Therefore although it is a human right, it is not a "natural" or a "legal" human right. For it is not a result of intrinsic deduction from nature (*physis*) vis-à-vis the legal order of the state (like "natural" rights), nor is it attainable through juridical systems of the state (like "legal" rights). Cf. Vladan Peršić, "Personhood and Nature: Orthodox Theological Reflection on Human Rights" [in Serbian], in *Raskršća* [*Crossroads: Studies in Greek and Christian Philosophy*] (Belgrade: Plato, 1996), 93–111.

59. This philokalic dictum is paradigmatically developed by G. Mandzaridis, *Orthodox Spiritual Life* [in Greek] (Thessalonica: P. Pournara, 1993), 13 passim.

60. The complex and often problematically opaque relations between state, civic society, nation, and religion cannot be thematized in detail within the limited scope of this presentation. Nevertheless, it is helpful to consult, for instance, John A. Hall, ed., *The State of the Nation: Ernest Gellner and the Theory of Nationalism* (Cambridge: Cambridge University Press, 1998).

61. Atanasije Jevtić, "St. Sava: The Žiča Sermon on True Faith" [in Serbian], in *Sveti Sava i Kosovski Zavet* [*St Sava and the Kosovo Covenant*] (Belgrade: SKZ, 1992).

62. At this point one cannot help remembering St. Peter's exclamation: "Lord, it is well [good, *kalon*] that we are here" (Matt. 17:4).

63. Zarko Vidović, "The Covenant as Original Principle of European History" [in Serbian], in *Suočenje pravoslavlja sa Evropom* [*Encounter of Orthodoxy with Europe*] (Cetinje: Svetigora 1997), 181–202.

64. Here self-governance, as inner instance, coincides with governance in and over the sphere of state and public society, as outer instance—the latter consisting in respect for sharing power under law, determination of responsibility, imposition of social justice, and so on—all of which binds sociopolitical justice to the justice one does to one's soul.

65. Our hermeneutic of the Žiča council projects *svetosavlje* as a form of authentic Orthodox Christendom historically contextualized among the Serbs, not necessarily in terms of "nationalism" (a nineteenth-century phenomenon). In other words, *svetosavlje* was not, and should not become, a quasi-Christian protrusion of bionationalism in Serbian ethnic terms. This does not necessarily imply the death sentence to the historic nation-state nor does it exclude the possibility for Christian patriotism. Rather, it calls for stricter delimiting of the spiritual from the national(istic), as well as for sociopolitical reconstruction in terms of civic inclusiveness and other correctives to nationalistic frenzy.

66. V. M. Radulović & N. M. Krstić, eds., "Orthodoxy and Politics" [in Serbian], *Gradac* 110 (1993); see esp. in that issue M. Petrović, "Positions and Rights of the Byzantine Emperor in the Church," and D. Bogdanović, "Political Philosophy of Medieval Serbia."

67. Irinej Bulovič, "Church and Politics" [in Serbian], in Radulović and Krstić, eds., "Orthodoxy and Politics" [in Serbian], *Gradac* 110 (1993).

68. The legacy of St. Sava is connected with historic forms of *svetosavlje*, but it is not reduced to them without discernment, particularly in view of certain instances of retroactive political and ideological misuse for base ends. There are at least two reasons for this. First, as stated by Bishop Jovan Mladenović of the Diocese of Šumadija, "St. Sava is great because it is his *Christ* that is great." This amplifies the words of blessed Justin (Popović) of Ćelije: "To be Orthodox in a 'svetosavian' way means to ceaselessly struggle against passions and sins in one's self and the world surrounding one"s self." *Svetosavlje kao filosofija života* [*Svetosavlje as Philosophy of Life*] (Valjevo: Ćelije, 1993), 75–88. Second, nationalism (*ethnophiletism*) was condemned as a form of heresy by the major council of eastern patriarchs in Constantinople in 1872.

69. This spirit, in a modern context, has been honored and developed by the legislators of the federal law of Serbia and Montenegro on religious freedom, as they have argued for an inclusive ("osmotic") and cooperational interpretation of the legal separation of state and church, superimposed by the principle of neutrality, that is, rejection of positing a "state religion." Cf. *Encounter between State and Church* [in Serbian] (Belgrade: Federal Secretariat for Faiths, 2003).

70. This distinction helps prevent "leaps into the other genus" whereby an entire church is subjected to accusational discourse for what subjects or parties may have done with its doctrine or in its name. I also have in mind Györgu Konràd's definition of accusational or hatred speech: "The essence of the speech of hatred consists in the fact that my troubles, i.e. the troubles of my community, are always presented by another community, that we ourselves are not guilty of our own troubles. That we are never guilty of anything." *Anti-politics: Essays and Articles* [Serbian, *Antipolitika: eseji i članci*] (Podgorica/Budva: Oktoih Grad Teatar, 1999), 399.

71. At that point the "silence" of God in Bosnia might reverse itself in terms of being a form of God's listening to our human predicament: Hence silence is the speech of God's hearing (*akoe*) itself! Cf. Ivan I. Soloviev, *The Silence of God: A Theology of Hearing* [Serbian, *Ćutanje Boga: teologija sluha*, trans. D. Ramadanski] (Pančevo: Sveske), 136–40.

72. A relevant and bold presentation of deconstructive readings against Balkanistic power discourse is given by Bogoljub Šijaković, *A Critique of Balkanistic Discourse: Contribution to the Phenomenology of Balkan "Otherness"* (Toronto: Serbian Literary Company, 2004).

73. Slavoj Žižek, *Less Love, More Hatred!* [Serbian, *Manje ljubavi—više mržnje! Ili, zašto je vredno boriti se za hrišćansko nasledje*, trans. R. Mastilović]

(Belgrade: Beogradski krug, 2001), 152. An illuminating analysis of Balkan and East European nationalism, in terms of a refusal of enjoyment (multilateral refusal of grace, I would say) is given in S. Žižek, *Tarrying with the Negative* (Durham, NC: Duke University Press, 1993), 200–239.

74. Maria Todorova, *Imagining the Balkans* (Oxford: Oxford University Press, 1997), 188 [Serbian, *Imaginarni Balkan* (Belgrade: XX Vek, 1999)]. Also helpful in this respect are Vesna Goldsworthy, *Inventing Ruritania: The Imperialism of the Imagination* (New Haven, CT: Yale University Press, 1998); and Larry Wolff, *Inventing Eastern Europe: The Map of Civilization on the Mind of the Enlightenment* (Stanford, CA: Stanford University Press, 1994).

75. The report in 2000 of the "Commission on the Future of Multi-Ethnic Britain" (established by the Runnymede Trust) drew attention to this in stating that, for people of Asian, African Caribbean, and African heritage, "The concept of Englishness often seems inappropriate, since to be English, as the term is in practice used, is to be white. Britishness is not ideal, but at least appears acceptable." A few lines further, however, the report went on to blur this distinction in its comment: "It is widely understood that Englishness, *and therefore by extension Britishness*, is racially coded" [emphasis added]. Commission on the Future of Multi-Ethnic Britain, *The Future of Multi-Ethnic Britain: The Parekh Report* (London: Profile Books, 2000), 38.

76. The often grudging nature of these changes is exemplified by one of the earliest, and most significant, pieces of legislation in the English process, the so-called Toleration Act of 1689. Its full title was *An Act for Exempting Their Majesties' Protestant Subjects Dissenting from the Church of England from the Penalties of Certain Laws.*

77. Cf. John Langan's contribution in chapter 2.

78. For example, Lord Scarman, in the judgment *Ex p. Choudhury* over the possible extension of the blasphemy law to cover Islam, declared: "The offence belongs to a group of criminal offences designed to safeguard the internal tranquillity of the kingdom." Cited in S. H. Bailey, D. J. Harris, and B. L. Jones, *Civil Liberties: Cases and Materials,* 4th ed. (London: Butterworth, 1995), 593.

79. The situation of Muslims born in Britain is somewhat different, as is that of British citizens who choose to embrace Islam. Despite their differing biographies, however, both still face the fundamental issue addressing migrants to Britain: that of choosing to continue living as Muslims in a non-Muslim context.

80. *al-Nisā'* 4:97, as translated by M. S. Abdel Haleem, *The Qur'ān: A New Translation* (Oxford: Oxford University Press, 2004), 60. The phrase "those who have wronged themselves" is traditionally interpreted as meaning "by living in a place where they are unable to practise their religion." Cf. likewise *al-'Ankabūt* 29:56; *al-Zumar* 39:10; and *al-Dhāriyāt* 51:48–51.

81. Abū Dā'ūd, *Sunan* 14:2639, trans. Ahmad Hasan, www.usc.edu/dept/MSA (accessed June 5, 2008).

82. Bukhārī, *Ṣaḥīḥ* vol. 58, p. 239 (no. 3638).

83. Or, at least, to use another traditional expression roughly equivalent to *dār al-islām*, as the *dār al-amān* ("House of Safety").

84. Another category sometimes referred to in this intermediate ground is that of *dār al-da'wa*, the "House of Invitation," where *da'wa* (sometimes also translated "mission") is understood in terms of outgoing cooperation with non-Muslims.

85. Cf. the essay by Michael Nazir-Ali earlier for a clear delineation of the main lines of this consensus and its theological foundations.

86. *Whitehouse v. Lemon* (1979), a prosecution brought against the editor and publishers of *Gay News* over a poem containing a homosexual fantasy on the dead body of Christ. *Ex p. Choudhury* (1991) was an unsuccessful attempt to invoke the blasphemy law in relation to Salman Rushdie's *Satanic Verses*. See Bailey, Harris, and Jones, *Civil Liberties*, 591–95.

87. *Mandla v. Dowell Lee* (1983) defined the relevant criteria for a group to qualify for protection ("A long shared history . . . a cultural tradition of its own"), criteria that were held to include the (religious) communities of Sikhism and Judaism. See Bailey, Harris, and Jones, *Civil Liberties*, 638–41.

88. A high profile example is the recently formed campaigning group *Christian Voice*. Their website (www.christianvoice.org.uk) includes a petition against both the introduction of a new law on religious hatred and the abolition of the current law on blasphemy.

89. The influential Barnabas Fund, for example, which highlights issues relating to Christians in Muslim countries, has mounted on their website (www.barnabasfund.org) a campaign against a religious hatred law that focuses almost entirely on questions of free speech, without mentioning the current blasphemy provisions.

90. On January 18, 2005, for example, leading figures from the Church of England, Roman Catholic Church, and Free Churches joined with representatives of other faith communities in issuing a statement welcoming

the government's plans to introduce legislation outlawing incitement to religious hatred. Text on the website of Churches Together in Britain and Ireland, www.ctbi.org.uk. The statement made no explicit reference to the law on blasphemy.

91. Cf. the analysis of a spectrum of "ideological types" according to which one community can view another developed in David Lochhead, *The Dialogical Imperative: A Christian Reflection on Inter Faith Encounter* (London: SCM, 1988). Lochhead distinguishes successively between (a) "isolation," (b) "hostility," (c) "competition," (d) "partnership," and (e) "dialogue." The first position I have described earlier falls largely within (a), though overlapping with (b); the second is predominantly of type (b), though sometimes veering into (c); the third variously occupies (c), (d), and (e). Cf. Lochhead, *Dialogical Imperative,* 3–29.

Chapter 2

༄

Seeking the Common Good

For Christians and for Muslims, religion is not just a question of belonging to a community; it is also a force that seeks to contribute to the transformation of society. Muslims and Christians alike know themselves to be mandated by divine imperatives, informed by divine values, which must be offered to the task of reshaping the world in which they live. It is questionable indeed whether the process of interpretation and application that enables this can be straightforward even in religiously homogeneous contexts; it certainly is much more complex in societies marked by both religious diversity and a measure of secularity. This chapter presents first a Muslim and then a Christian discussion of the theological underpinnings of this, followed by four locally contextualized studies of governance and justice.

Tariq Ramadan emphasizes the variety of ways in which Muslims seek to move from the text of the Qur'an and the Sunna to the contemporary context. He argues that it is possible to trace a continuity in the values of justice and self-governance between the individual and the collective; building on this, there is general agreement among Muslims that the state has a responsibility to protect basic rights, that the Islamic collective must be regulated by law, and that proper governance involves consultation. However, Ramadan goes on to distinguish three clearly different ways in which Muslims apply these general principles to concrete situations—respectively, literalism, reformism, and the shaping of new models to embody underlying Islamic principles in new contexts. As a Muslim living in a minority situation, he indicates that the last approach—which he favors—can, if taken seriously, imply a major redefinition of the fundamental category of Shari'a.

John Langan explores from a Roman Catholic perspective the meaning and relevance of the concept of "common good." He points out that, while this generally refers to issues of law and public policy when used in social discourse, it also in Christian understanding has a continuity with the "spiritual goods" of redemption and salvation. Like Ramadan, Langan maps disagreement within his own faith, as well as indicating clearly where his own theological preference lies. Thus he acknowledges that many Christians have historically chosen, as some still do, to adopt an adversarial approach to differences in society; nevertheless, he insists that adversarialism will not provide an adequate or appropriate resource for Christians seeking to engage with a mixed society. Recognizing that religiously mandated traditions do face a challenge in handling their own convictions of normative supremacy in societies where these are controverted by others, Langan offers an interesting map of possible ways to address this in a catalogue of possible relations between "politics" and "religion." It is significant to note that in this typology a strict separation between the two is only one of several options, and that not the most viable.

Despite their very different presentations, Ramadan and Langan do have some tendencies in common. Both locate their discussions of governance and justice within wider theological discourses with which the former display conceptual continuities. Both acknowledge, though, that it is not possible simply to read off a program for society from the datum of the religious tradition; indeed, both chart strong disagreements within their respective faiths over the very methodologies that might be available to move from theology to social policy. Further layers of complexity are introduced into these debates when onto these underlying theological disagreements there are overlaid the diverse historical and cultural parameters of the various local contexts within which Christians and Muslims live and meet, as is demonstrated by the four case studies that follow.

Fikret Karcic presents three extracts showing the views of leading Bosnian Muslims on the relation between religion and political power—views that over a long period, from the Ottomans onward, developed piecemeal through focused religious responses to particular practical issues. Writing from the same geographical context but from a different religious and cultural community, Vladimir Ciric describes both the problems and the possibilities that arise from what he describes as an Eastern "personalist" approach shared by Muslims and Orthodox Christians. Mohammad Hashim Kamali describes in some detail the provisions made for different religious communities within the constitutional framework of modern Malaysia and explains the extent to which the affirmation of minority participation this involves is sustained by a commitment on the part of the majority to an inclusive vision of "civilizational Islam" (*Islām hadhārī*). John Azumah demonstrates how in West Africa many Muslims will regard secular democracy as a Christian construct and express a preference for living under Shari'a; conversely, any such moves toward the Islamization of society will be viewed with grave concern by Christians. He concludes with a plea that Muslims and Christians should make themselves better informed about what either is commending to the other as a model for governance and justice; this emphasis on the need for careful attention to the other's viewpoint is indeed echoed by all the contributors to this chapter.

Islamic Views of the Collective

&

Tariq Ramadan

This essay is arranged in three parts.[1] First is an introduction about the upstream conditions for the Islamic message and how we deal with governance and justice from an Islamic perspective—not merely of one Muslim but of the whole Islamic community. It is essential to understand that we have different views and approaches on this topic. The second discusses the fundamental principles found in the Islamic tradition. The third and concluding part explains three main ways of understanding this Islamic view. I do not wish to give the impression that we have a common viewpoint on these issues or an agreed view of justice; I want to convey from an Islamic viewpoint that we are dealing with an intracommunity debate about these issues. To talk only about general principles is not helpful when we deal with practical questions in the West or in Muslim majority countries. I end with my perspective about an ethical way of dealing with this issue.

Islam and the Collective: Agreements and Disagreements

First, there is common agreement among Muslims that in Islam there is a very strong message and teaching as to the direction of the human collective. This is something that is a spiritual teaching at an individual level, but it is also a very clear and strong message as to how we should deal with collective affairs, the public sphere. This common agreement is based on the objective of the message, the purpose for which the message has been revealed. At one point there is a clear parallel between what is asked at the individual level and what is asked at the collective level. At the individual level, what is the objective of a spiritual life? First, to please Him, the One. Why? Because he is God, the Creator. How? By following the principles and the teachings, the objectives of which are to govern yourself in a balanced and just way. This self-governance is a way of dealing with your own heart and mind. You are responsible for your own heart, and not everything in your heart is good. You are given responsibilities as well as rights; you should know your duties and your rights, seeking harmony with yourself based on the specific concept of *jihād* (or "struggle"). The aim here is to resist that which is bad in your heart and to promote that which is good, because you are trying to reach inner justice. We need to try to find justice within ourselves, to govern ourselves. This is an exact parallel at the individual level to the challenge at the collective level of trying to find a balanced approach with individual rights and duties to the collective. God loves justice, and the spiritual personal life is a mirror of the spiritual collective organization. There must be consistency between the way we deal with our own self and the way we seek equity and balance in society. These are commonly agreed points, but there are also disagreements among Muslims, very deep and strong disagreements.

All Muslims rely on the Qur'ān and the Sunna, but they disagree on the number of verses and *ahadīth* that deal with the collective and on the nature of prescriptions. This is a major disagreement. Scholars will say variously that there are more than a thousand, or more than six hundred, or less than two hundred such verses. The more verses of this kind you admit, the less scope there is for rationality or creative judgment. The question "Which are the verses dealing with the collective sphere?" is thus very important. We also disagree on the nature of Islamic prescriptions and rules: Are these absolute, or can they to be contextualized? It is not possible to understand how Muslims speak about governance without recognizing this disagreement among them about both the number and the nature of collective verses. A third major disagreement involves the nature of the connection between revealed text, rational interpretation, and context. When we deal with governance, we deal with interpretations and specific contexts as well as with texts. The deepest disagreements are here. To understand what is happening in the Islamic world and among Western Muslims now, it is important to understand these three disagreements: about the number of texts, about the nature of the texts, and about the nature of the connections of the texts with interpretations and contexts. Different trends appear around these in Islamic communities: a literalist approach, a reformist approach, and a rationalist approach, each dealing with the sources in different ways.

Discussions between Muslims and Christians should not go straight to global issues. We need to be pragmatic in the way we are dealing with these different approaches. We are living in common pluralistic societies, and we need to understand the differences within ourselves, our own internal struggles. If we are to build bridges with one another, we need to understand what we are fighting about within our own communities. The common agreement among Muslims and the various disagreements can all be encompassed under one common concept: namely, how we understand the notion of Shari'a. Many Muslims now will not use the word *Shari'a* because they are concerned it will be misunderstood, but it remains a central concept. One traditional understanding of it is as "a way, a path": the way you are trying to remain faithful to the Islamic messages. But there is also a very strong legacy from the *fuqaha* saying that the Shari'a is basically a set of rules. There is also disagreement as to what is part of the Shari'a. There is a widely accepted and important difference between *fiqh*, meaning the interpretation and application of the law (or jurisprudence), and Shari'a, in the sense of a set of global principles. However, this does not in itself serve to define the Shari'a, though it does make clearer what it is not. This is a central issue in the way that Muslims speak about and deal with the collective sphere.

General Islamic Principles on the Collective Sphere

The second part of this essay deals with the question of what teaching is found within the Islamic tradition regarding the public sphere. For Muslims, this also is extracted from the Qur'an and the Sunna, from the prophetic experience in a specific limited period of time, and afterward also from the successors and the Rightly Guided Caliphs. From these historical experiences and from the scriptural sources, the *ulamā* have tried to extract a global message for the collective sphere. There are issues here essential in the perception of Islamic law and jurisprudence, which have been understood by the scholars who deal with *uṣūl al-fiqh*, the fundamentals of the religious teachings.

First, in relation to the global sphere, there is teaching as to what should be protected in a specific collectivity, in a specific society. From the Qur'an and the Sunna are extracted the principal objectives that should be protected and implemented. In Islamic tradition, these are identified as the five (or six) main principles or objectives (*maqāṣid*): the protection of, respectively, *dīn* (religion), *nafs* (personal integrity), *'aql* (intellect), *nasl* (everything that is connected with the family, its ties and relations), and property (*māl*).[2] These words can indeed be found in the Qur'ān, but their categorization in this way is not Qur'ānic; it represents a project by the *ulamā* to extract from the sources a general perspective of *al-maqāṣid al-ḍarūriyya*, the essential objectives of the sources. At this point, we can understand two things. First, it is the responsibility of an organized collectivity, state, or government to protect these five (or six) principles. By recognizing that the objective of the Shari'a or the scriptural sources is to direct us toward these principles, we also recognize that we have rights to be protected, and the state or government has a responsibility to protect these fundamental rights. This is an important point regarding the way that justice is understood in relation to individuals at the collective level.

Second, in relation to collective affairs, there can be extracted from the Qur'ān and from the prophetic experience two important factors. The first of these is that there is no structured collectivity not relying on law. It is indeed disputable as to whether the legal framework of Medina can be described as being based on the first constitution, but it is at least certain that our collectivity should be based on a framework that is based on a very clear understanding that laws are among us, that our interpersonal relationships are governed by a state of law. The second factor is the central and global principle of *shūrā*, consultation or deliberation. There are just two Qur'ānic verses referring to this:

> [Those who] conduct their affairs by mutual consultation (*amruhum shūrā baynahum*). (al-Shūrā 42:38)
>
>   Consult with them about matters (*shāwirhum fil-amr*). (Āl 'Imrān 3:159)

In the collective sphere, the Prophet is commended to consult with the community. This is a general concept; governance is not a matter of one's personal choice alone but involves consultation. This has been understood from the beginning and is shown by many instances. For example, just before Badr, a companion, went to the Prophet and asked, "Is this place your choice, or has it been revealed to you by revelation?" and the Prophet said, "It is my choice, not by revelation." The companion replied, "If it is your choice, you are wrong; we have to move the place to one that is strategically better." Here there can be seen the making of a distinction between revelation and rational or individual decision, between the Prophet and the man. Governance is about a human being trying to deal with the collective sphere.

There are two general spheres. In relation to the duties of government and in relation to the rights of the individual, *al-maqāṣid al-ḍarūriyya* leads to a recognition of rights; for the collectivity, there is a need for law and for consultation. We need to be involved in the way we are governing ourselves and making decisions. It is only in this way, through relying on the first sphere and following the rules prescribed in relation to the second sphere, that justice can be achieved. It is important also to realize that the principles in this tradition are beyond the results. In particular, the second verse relating to *shūrā* was revealed after a defeat of the Muslims.[3] It is after this that the Prophet is commanded to consult his community at the same time that he is enjoined to forgive them for their disobedience. *Shūrā* is thus presented as a principle to be followed regardless of the result. The principle must be followed whatever its consequences. This may not mean that you are going to be right, but you have to be faithful. There can be a right to be wrong through following this principle.

At this level of general principles, everything can be agreed, but in the historical experiences of Muslims the principles come to be understood in very different ways. Indeed, while the general principles are fine, it is possible for the way in which they are historically applied to be very destructive, in the sense that they end up contrary to the general objectives. I describe three different understandings of this in the following section.

Three Ways of Applying Islamic Principles

The first understanding considers that from the Qur'an, the prophetic experience, and the Rightly Guided Caliphs there are available both the principles and the right models. In order to be faithful to the principles, it is necessary to duplicate these models. Muslims must return to what the Prophet and the Caliphs did, in the way that they did it. Thus the principles are understood not in a universal sense but according to the way in which they were historically implemented. According to this argument, the principle that "the authority comes from God" (*al ḥaqq min al-illah*) means that the principles must be implemented only in the way that they were in the time of the Prophet and the Caliphs. To follow this route is the only way to be faithful, because it means that one is not following one's personal choice or being guided by one's historical circumstances, but instead one is recognizing the absoluteness of the message. This is the understanding in the literalist tradition and in some political Islamic movements. Much discussion has centered on the verse *al-ḥaqq min al-illah*—is this verse to be repeated, to be interpreted, and to be connected to history in order to understand its history? For example, Ḥizb-ut-Taḥrir are among the groups in several countries now grappling with these issues and maintaining that this particular historical structure is the pattern for universal faithfulness. In this view, the historical models are part of the principles. Thus, as soon as somebody says that he or she can be faithful to a state that does not exactly follow the structure that was realized at the start of Islamic history, that person is thereby being unfaithful to Islam. Unbelief, perversity, and injustice are seen as linked.

A second pattern of understanding is the reformist approach, which can appear in various forms. According to this, the principles are again extracted from the sources, but according to a specific understanding that this is adaptable to history within certain limits, often influenced by Mawdūdī. The model here still forms part of the principles, in that the language is still that of an Islamic state, a structure that exists in the historical reality of Muslims. Or is this "Islamic state" something that is still to be, yet to be created out of the principles of the Islamic tradition? This form of reformism very often refuses any new kind of vocabulary regarding democracy as a problematic concept because it does not come out of an Islamic source. Thus the language of "shuro-cracy," for example, was coined in Algeria, trying to indicate thereby something close to democracy but yet remaining specifically Islamic. However, it is difficult to understand what this actually means. Issues of terminology can be very telling in indicating the approach that is being taken to questions of government and authority. Among the majority of Muslims and Islamic movements now, democracy is not seen as a problem; but there is another concept to be addressed, which is that of citizenship. All this terminology comes from outside the Islamic tradition and so poses the challenge of how it is to be understood from that perspective.

Third, there is an approach that involves extracting the principles from, while being careful not to confuse them with, the historical experiences. Once the principle is extracted, a model must then be sought for it, and the appropriate terminology and concepts must be defined. So long as they are in keeping with the fundamental principles, it is possible to use new terminology. For example, in speaking of "citizenship" it is no longer necessary to use the expression *dhimmī*. When the principles have been extracted, it is necessary to rely not solely on the scriptures and sources but on the exercise of collective rationality. This is a central issue in speaking of governance and justice.

In summary, it is important to recognize the extent of the deep disagreements between Muslims over these questions. What we can say is that the state has obligations to ensure the protection of fundamental objectives. The state has an ethical obligation. This recognition of the duties of the state in turn implies that the sources can be read in such a way as to imply that individuals have rights—for example, in relation to the essential right to freedom of speech. There is no alternative in developing this but to rely on a state of law, although Muslims will not easily agree about the source of those laws. From this and from the practice of *shūrā*, for me, there flow four key points: equality of citizenship, a principle that can be validated through the Sunna; universal suffrage, which relies on an understanding of *shūrā* as being deliverable through elections; accountability, the principle of which can be found in the scriptural text; and a reliance on rational, ethical, and creative political thought. This is often missing in the way Muslims approach the Shari'a today, but for me, as a Muslim living in a minority in another society, everything in that society that is just should be seen as itself part of Shari'a. Shari'a is not an exclusive concept: Everything that promotes right governance falls within its scope, as we do not have an exclusive model to which we must confine ourselves.

The Common Good

Catholicism, Pluralism, and Secular Society

∾

John Langan

Concern for the common good is one of the characteristic features of Catholic social thought; the notion has roots in the classical world and in Augustine and Aquinas, but it achieved a special prominence in Catholic social teaching over the last century. This social teaching is embodied in a series of documents beginning with the encyclical *Rerum novarum* of Leo XIII (1891) and continuing through the extensive writings of John Paul II. It also includes the apostolic constitution, *Gaudium et spes*, "The Church and the Modern World" (1965), and numerous documents of the various conferences of bishops over the last forty years, with particular importance being given to the statements of the Latin American bishops at Medellin and Puebla in 1968 and 1979 and to the two pastoral letters of the U.S. Catholic bishops on "The Challenge of Peace" (1983) and "Economic Justice for All" (1986). But our reflections on this topic should not be simply about how one religious tradition develops its thought about a fundamental notion of social ethics. We need to recognize that the notion of the common good is an essential part of how modern Catholicism presents itself to the wider world and that this notion demands critical scrutiny from people who stand in other religious and intellectual traditions. We should also acknowledge that the notion has a complex life outside Catholicism and that many people use the notion without any idea of its religious connections and uses.

In this essay I begin by reflecting briefly on the meaning of "common good" and then stating some challenges that contemporary secular thought and Islam might in their different ways wish to put to the Catholic notion of the common good. Next I pay particular attention to the adversarial challenge to the Catholic way of understanding the common good, as this ordinarily involves according a privileged status to a particular religious tradition. I conclude with a review of the main ways of resolving the resulting tension.

The expression "common good" combines two highly positive elements: the idea of what is shared by a community and the idea of what is desirable and worthwhile in itself. It evokes our hopes for agreement and our desire for highly valued forms of satisfaction and fulfillment. It points to our yearning for a peaceful and harmonious community capable of enjoying the fullness of peace. Why then is it not irresistible in its appeal?

The first answer to this question is that the notion is highly generic and unlimited. The adjective *good* itself is the most commonly used term in the English language to express approval, to commend things and persons, to evaluate and select among a range of options. We speak of good roads, knives, golf clubs, apple trees, barbers, and trumpeters. We recognize different kinds of good: valor and victory in war, knowledge and wisdom in our mental life, compassion and patience in our relationships, economic success and rare commodities, infrastructure and technology as the basis for our complex forms of cooperation, aesthetically excellent objects and performances, and objects that we treasure for their personal meaning or their historical connections. Goods can be material, spiritual, moral, aesthetic, commercial, useful, instrumental, intrinsic, personal, social, private, or public. The term is pervasive and has different implications in different contexts. In the language of scholastic philosophy and theology, "good" (*bonum*) is a transcendental notion that is to be understood analogically—that is, with a meaning that is partly the same and partly different across the range of its applications. Its very diversity is meant to be brought into a complex order of goods (*ordo bonorum*). In many, perhaps most, contemporary settings, "good" is interpreted in a subjective and individualistic way; that is to say, "X is good" means "X is what I think is good" and "X is what is to my advantage." Such an interpretation of "good," while nearly axiomatic in vast stretches of Western bourgeois society, is clearly alien to the formative tradition of Christianity and, I suspect, to Islam as well.

"Common," which is a somewhat less positive term, does serve as a corrective to this individualistic view of "good." The belief that at least some of those goods that are common have a certain priority over individual goods and are indispensable fits nicely with the Aristotelian and Thomistic view that the human person is by nature social or political. The "common good" clearly seems to be a notion that belongs in the realms of law and public policy even though it also keeps connections with basic issues in ethical theory. But we should remember that it is not confined to these practical realms. For the idea of the "common good" applies within the spiritual and theological realms. It is an essential part of Christian doctrine that our destiny as fallen and redeemed creatures is something that we share, regardless of our personal histories and preferences. Despite the strong contemporary tendency to treat religion as a private realm in which personal preference is expected to be dominant, Christian theology has maintained that the goods of redemption and salvation are in a fundamental sense part of our common history as God's children. They are available to all, they cannot be appropriated to the exclusion of others, they are in some sense multiplied by missionary activity and by other ways of expanding the faith community, and they are not differentiated or diminished by being shared by different persons. In the Christian view, the spiritual goods enjoyed and transmitted by individuals are moments of participation in goods that are eternal in their source and that are freely given by that source. They lie outside what Hume and Rawls discuss as "the circumstances of justice." But they are not beyond the reach of human concern and decision, as these must be present if these goods are to be actually enjoyed by human beings. The common character of these ultimately important goods should always be kept in mind as we look at goods that can be recognized across theological lines but that are more likely to be contested and divisive in social and economic realms.

There are three problems in the notion of the common good that make its acceptance and implementation difficult. They can all be readily surmised from my previous remarks on the two key terms. The first is that the notion of common good, because of the range and qualitative differences of the goods that can be included in it, is an incoherent notion that will only serve to confuse policy discussions and decisions about the allocation of resources. Even its critics will admit that the notion of the common good has a certain emotive power and serves to give a rhetorical advantage to those who use it. But in the minds of the critics, it suffers from the incoherence attaching to the notion of the general happiness or welfare in the utilitarian tradition; this incoherence is expanded because of the greater range and diversity of goods about which the religious traditions are concerned. The notion of the common good attempts to bring together too many different kinds of things for us to be able to make rational choices among them. We would have to measure and assess outcomes along too many different axes if we were to attempt this sort of decision. We would end up conflating the desires and choices of disparate individuals, and we would confuse the task of social choice with the rational evaluation of alternatives by individuals. This is a line of argument that has considerable power if we attempt to use the notion of the common good as a kind of decision procedure for setting and evaluating law and public policy. It should be noted that it is endorsed by some prominent Christian ethical and legal theorists who are highly critical of approaches that involve comparing and aggregating goods of diverse sorts.

The second line of criticism against the notion of the common good is that it is a threat to the practice of human rights, especially the rights of individuals. For evidence of this one can look at the teaching of Thomas Aquinas on the topic of capital punishment. St. Thomas offers a justification of this practice on the grounds of the common good with no reference to the rights of the individual who is to be punished.[4] He uses the analogy of a gangrenous limb that is removed for the sake of the survival of the whole being. This analogy has the reassuring implication that the person to be punished is guilty—or is, in his language, a malefactor. The criticism sometimes made of utilitarianism that it could be invoked to justify the punishment of the innocent or the surrender of hostages to an aggressor would not apply to St. Thomas's position. But it is not clear that he has a considered defense against the charge that his approach will tilt the balance in favor of the state against the individual. This was a problem that was addressed in the twentieth century by the distinguished neo-Thomist Jacques Maritain, who had witnessed the development of totalitarian systems that oppressed individuals for the sake of the community or the state and that had found sympathetic adherents within such traditionally Catholic cultures as Italy and France. Maritain's way of dealing with this problem was to incorporate the human rights of individuals into the conception of the common good itself. In this he was building on Thomas's own realization that the lives of the innocent were an inherent part of the common good and that regimes or political movements that attacked the innocent would necessarily damage the common good. The Catholic notion of the common good is not itself a form of totalitarian or fascist social theory, but it does need to be distinguished from the more idealistic aspects of such theories and from social ideologies that extol heroic sacrifices that are less than voluntary. It becomes a matter of great importance to understand the relation between the common good and individual rights and choices in such a way that it is not a zero-sum game, in which whatever advances the rights of individuals diminishes the common good and whatever enhances the common good requires a subordination of the rights of individuals. This is not to say that the rights of individuals can never be subordinated to the common good—a position that would commit us to a form of individualism that would be incompatible with the major religious traditions and with the practical demands of public life.

A third line of criticism against the notion of the common good is based on the views of various conservative religious thinkers, both Christian and Muslim. Briefly, it is that the notion is overly ecumenical, that it requires us to find a place in our social ethics for the interests and the concerns of those who are "the enemies of God." In this approach, the contrast between good and evil, between the elect and the damned, between the friends of God and the enemies of God, is and should be prior to the elaboration of moral norms and political structures open to the entire society. In this adversarial and exclusive approach, harms to the enemies of God do not diminish the common good; they may, in fact, even enhance it. The community whose well-being is to be promoted is defined as the community of those who have accepted God's offer of the covenant and salvation, those who have chosen "the path of life" over "the path of death." Efforts to promote a common good that overlook the fundamental difference between those who have accepted God's offer and those who have either ignored or rejected it are bound to be incoherent and to lead to spiritual confusion, tolerance of evil, loss of faith, and idolatry. Forming a fundamental community with the enemies of God is impossible, though a provisional and temporary modus vivendi may of course be established.

Now this may strike Christian readers as an indirect way of characterizing the approach of radical Islam—how accurate such a judgment would be I cannot say. But I think that Christians should be ready to acknowledge that until quite recent times most Christians and most Christian societies have relied on such an adversarial conception. They should also recognize that this position, though currently unfashionable, is not very far from the views of St. Augustine, particularly his definition of a republic and the contrast he makes between the city of God and the city of man.[5] In such an approach, an adversarial conception of humanity and its projects, or more accurately God's projects for it, is given priority over the goods appropriate to a mixed community of the sort commonly found in the world or in our actual political experience. A mixed society, as I am using the term here, is one that is not defined in terms of its agreement on ultimate values and ends but arises as the result of a complex history and imperfect voluntary associations. Such a society is more coherent than a mere juxtaposition of different ethnic groups occupying one territory, but it is not founded on a shared ideology or set of values or on what John Rawls would discuss as a "comprehensive conception of the good." The unity of such a society may be quite imperfect, but it is itself an important good whose absence in "failed states" turns them into centers of suffering and crime for their one-time citizens and for large numbers of their neighbors. Most of the states in the contemporary world are mixed states in this sense.

In the adversarial conception, there is likely to be a strong commitment to the establishment of a community of the saints or the justified, a community that is called to be faithful under persecution and to be victorious in the long term. In such a community religious agreement is taken to be a fundamental good that should not be lightly diminished. When the adversary is characterized as a nonearthly or spiritual power (Satan, demons, false gods, "powers and principalities"), the conflict is especially likely to be conceived in stark terms that do not admit of a middle ground, as the primary antagonists are conceived in ways that do not allow for the complexity and ambiguity of ordinary human motivation. We do not expect the devil and his allies and subordinates to have mixed motives. If the primary form of conflict is eschatological, there is a considerable temptation to devalue present losses and sufferings in comparison with the promised gains and threatened losses of the end time and eternity. The famous story of the inquisitor who was asked whether nonheretical prisoners should be spared, and who replied that all were to be killed because God would save his own, is an appropriate illustration of how this tendency of thought can work.[6] In the hands of utopian visionaries and revolutionaries, this way of giving priority to adversarial over cooperative conceptions of the common good can be used to justify the infliction of enormous sacrifices on groups that are seen as belonging temporarily or permanently to "the dark side." This is one of the themes of Peter Berger's *Pyramids of Sacrifice* and has figured prominently in Marxist efforts to reconcile ideal generosity and practical cruelty in a way that offers some possibility of justification for the policies of such revolutionary leaders as Lenin, Stalin, Mao Tse-tung, and Pol Pot. It also figures in a different way in the justification of the colonial imposition of religious and moral values on people who were thought of as being under the domination of Satan or as lacking the capacity to understand right and wrong through their own capacities.

A character in *Things Fall Apart* by Chinua Achebe, a novel that deals with the coming of Christianity to the Ibos in Nigeria at the end of the nineteenth century, exemplifies this pattern of thought in its colonial and imperial form in the late Victorian period: "Mr. Brown's successor was the Reverend James Smith, and he was a different kind of man. He condemned openly Mr. Brown's policy of compromise and accommodation. He saw things as black and white. And black was evil. He saw the world as a battlefield in which the children of light were locked in mortal conflict with the sons of darkness. He spoke in his sermons about sheep and goats and about wheat and tares. He believed in slaying the prophets of Baal."[7] Someone who believes in the adversarial conception need not be an advocate of persecution or violence; it may be enough to achieve separation or a subordination or marginalization of the opposing elements in society. Furthermore, it seems that the adversarial view commits its proponent to affirm a fundamental inequality between the beliefs and interests of those who belong to the community of the elect and those who are not included. The inequality of status for the two groups on opposite sides of the great religious divide is illustrated in the old Catholic maxim "Error has no rights."

Adversarialism can be thought of as a consciously adopted position forming part of a theoretical view of religion and society, but it can also be a tendency in one's social perceptions and beliefs and valuations that is not consciously adopted but that still can have an influence that is all the more powerful for its not being consciously attended to. Adversarialism is an attitude that can and sometimes does find powerful expression in prejudicial policies, in political advocacy, and in violent actions by individuals and groups. In examining the adversarial views and attitudes of religious groups, we are not merely looking at a problematic element in a theoretical position; we are also examining something that can be enormously destructive to social cohesion, to the human rights of the less powerful, and to the stability and security of society. These different levels and forms of adversarialism are logically, and to some extent practically, distinct from each other. It would surely be a naïve observer who thought a Vatican document or a World Council of Churches document rejecting adversarial theological views would ensure the disappearance of adversarialism from the attitudes and the behavior of, for instance, the Catholics and Protestants of Northern Ireland or the Maronites of Lebanon.

Is it possible to show in some clear and conclusive way that the adversarial conception is wrong and that it must yield to more inclusive conceptions? Is it possible to do this in a way that does not dismiss the truth claims of major religious traditions and that does not involve the subordination of these traditions to secular conceptions that may seem appropriate in mixed societies but that seem repugnant to many of the sincerely devout who have a strong preference for living in a community of the just? I cannot offer a quick and easy answer to this problem, which is, I think, a most urgent normative problem for interreligious dialogue and for international security. The core of the difficulty is that participants in this debate are in disagreement about fundamental premises on the source and weight of religious authority, on the relationship between faith and reason, on the basic principles of a just constitution, on acceptable methods for interpreting authoritative religious texts and for applying them to various contemporary social settings, and on the ways in which religious doctrine admits of development. But if we focused only on the many forms and areas of disagreement, we would be driven into the intellectually and pragmatically unsatisfactory incoherence of relativism.

But I do think that we can offer some considerations that will mitigate what would be for many the painful choice between religious traditionalism and secular rationality and civility as guides to the structuring of society. First, we can acknowledge that the shaping of a community of the elect conceived primarily in religious terms is a legitimate possibility even in Western pluralistic and secular societies. Normally this involves some degree of withdrawal from the larger society and a renunciation (explicit or implicit) of any attempt to rule or control the larger society. Religious communities ranging from Benedictine monasteries to Mennonite groups, from Hindu ashrams to perfectionist communes, from Mormon states to Shaker settlements, have proceeded in this way and have in the course of the twentieth century found secular imitators as well. The withdrawing group can set boundaries within which its members voluntarily submit to its principles and norms, but it is not free to employ coercion against recalcitrant members, though it may expel them. Even less may it use coercion against those who have chosen not to join it.

Second, a religious society or community, whether it is located on the margins of society or at the center of the public square, may use persuasion to attract others into membership or to convince them of the moral necessity of adopting some of its principles. This sort of thing goes on routinely in most Western democracies. In Europe and in Latin America there have been explicitly religious political parties, though many of them have fallen into decline in the last fifteen years (e.g., the Christian Democrats in Italy). These parties have normally been open to members who do not share the religious faith that was a founding impulse of the party, but they have also been quite open about proposing legislation affirming and applying religious values.

Those who propose a very strict separation of politics and religion often fail to recognize how difficult it is to maintain this separation between two great overlapping areas of human concern. It is important to bear in mind that this is a far broader project than the separation between church and state, which is between two distinct institutions, institutions that in their elaborated form are characteristic of Western civilization and that are not precisely paralleled elsewhere. The inescapable difficulty that stands in the way of achieving the total separation of religion and politics is that religious people have rights to freedom of speech and association and political action that they may choose to exercise in ways that extend beyond the limits of secular expectations and that manifest a desire to eliminate the dualism of social norms taken as axiomatic by the separationists. Furthermore, the actual exercise of rights of political participation by the religious need not always have as its primary goal or principal result an increase in the power of religious institutions and groups. The most widely recognized example of this point is provided by the U.S. civil rights movement, in which religious leaders, most notably but far from exclusively the Reverend Dr. Martin Luther King Jr., opened up opportunities for oppressed African Americans regardless of their religious affiliations and with the assistance of a wide range of organizations, both religious and nonreligious. It would clearly be invidious and unfair for proponents of secularism and liberalism to accept this sort of religious involvement in Western polities and to deny similar possibilities to Islamic groups whether in the West or in the Islamic world. It is to be expected and accepted as legitimate that various religious groups will use the freedom of the public space in democratic societies to advocate policies that they believe are required by justice and that bear the mark of their religious inspiration.

The most satisfactory way of dealing with this problem is not through imposing the dictates and practices of a secularist regime on multitudes of more or less resistant believers but rather by finding within the religious tradition itself considerations that lead to the recognition of a common humanity in all the groups of a religiously mixed society and to the acceptance of religious freedom and the rights of conscience. I can affirm that it took Catholicism a long time to arrive at this position and to abandon the effort to impose a single normative regime on Western Christianity. In the course of the nineteenth and twentieth centuries many particular steps were taken, but the principled acceptance of the idea and the practice of religious freedom only came with Vatican II's document *Dignitatis humanae* in 1965. But it was necessary to over-come serious internal opposition within the Catholic theological tradition before this outcome could be reached. From the late eighteenth century we can trace significant moves within the Catholic community to accept the principle of religious freedom. But these moves were often coerced by revolutionary forces or were opportunistic responses to changes made by other societies that were learning the benefits of affirming religious freedom as a principle even when it conflicted with their previous principles and prejudices. As a result, Catholicism went through a period where it was both the beneficiary and the opponent of religious freedom.

In sum, there seem to be four major ways of dealing with the contention for normative supremacy among religious and ideological traditions and com-munities. These are (a) to affirm one tradition to the exclusion of all others, (b) to affirm one tradition along with the clear subordination of other traditions and communities, (c) to modify one tradition in such a way that human rights to religious freedom and to equal respect can be affirmed as commitments of principle, and (d) to impose certain "rules of the game" (which can be pre-sented as legal requirements to be justified democratically or pragmatically or as conclusions from a philosophical position). The first is the position of religious fundamentalism and exclusivism of the sort fostered for a long time in Catholic Spain as well as in significant parts of the Islamic world (such as Saudi Arabia). I take the second to be the position of the main Sunni tradition as well as of those European countries that had established churches (which could be Angli-can, Lutheran, Orthodox, Calvinist, as well as Catholic) along with toleration for specified minority religious groups and movements. The current Russian regime seems to be offering an updated version of this position. The second often involves restrictions on religious freedom and inequalities in treatment, but it does not ordinarily challenge religious freedom in general or lead to active persecution. The third developed gradually within the Protestant cultures of the North Atlantic and then in a belated but more explicit way in Roman Catholicism in the second half of the twentieth century. The fourth has been a favored position for revolutionaries anxious to remove religious establishments (as in France in 1789 and Russia in 1917), for philosophers and theologians keen to criticize and revise religious traditions, and for those politicians and intellectuals along with assorted military and business leaders who are commonly labeled as modernizers, Westernizers, or liberals. This fourth is commonly presented as a work of reason, a reason that has been stripped of religious and traditional vestments and that is common to all suitably disposed persons. The approach taken in the fourth may rely on intuitively known universal principles or it may arrive at principles that self-interested rational persons choose to adopt in order to enhance their interests and to keep the peace.

If we look at these positions in pragmatic terms, we can see that the first is incompatible with full and open participation in a pluralistic world. Implementing it requires extensive restrictions on trade, immigration, and communication as well as an extensive and intrusive apparatus for the monitoring and control of those who would challenge the established normative tradition. It puts the state that adopts it into a stance of permanent confrontation with the normative structure of the *oikoumene*, which is unavoidably pluralistic. In most parts of the world, the fourth is experienced as a kind of extrinsic criticism that is not well connected to the basic religious orientation of the public. This is true even in a country such as the United States, which has had a constitutionally mandated separation of church and state since 1791. The fourth has the attraction of being reached by a straightforward line of argument without getting tangled in the details of religious history and religious claims; but this is also its vulnerability, as it can readily be described as dismissive and disrespectful of religion. The second is sustainable for long periods of time, as history shows, but comes under pressure as populations become more diverse and religion loses many of its traditional constituencies. The third then becomes important and attractive because it offers the prospect of a regime that affirms religious freedom and equal respect for all even while it roots this in a religious interpretation of life and morality. It gives religious people religious reasons for following policies that foster a great civic good (religious freedom and peace); it gives nonreligious people some assurance that they can regard the religious commitments of their neighbors with equanimity and respect. This outcome can itself be a significant contribution to the common good. How this goal is to be reached through the internal development of Islam is not a matter on which I am competent to pronounce but about which I am anxious to learn and for which I earnestly pray.

Bosnian Muslim Scholars
on Governance and Justice

૬⁄ઝ

Fikret Karcic

In modern Islamic thought in Bosnia and Herzegovina, developed in post-Ottoman times, there was no systematic treatment of issues such as governance and justice. Bosnian scholars of the Habsburg era, 1878–1918, initiated debates about the permissibility of Muslims staying in a non-Muslim polity, about Muslims serving in a non-Muslim army, about the compatibility of being Muslim and being European, and the like. These issues were debated in the form of responses (*fatwā*) and short treatises. The same trend continued during the Kingdom of Yugoslavia, 1918–41. During Socialist rule in Bosnia and Herzegovina, 1945–90, Bosnian Muslim scholars faced new challenges centered on the question of how to preserve Muslim identity in a Marxist secular state. The elaboration of an Islamic view on governance and justice was unlikely to take place in a situation when the regime considered that only the private life of individuals is a legitimate area of religion. During the breakup of Yugoslavia and the genocidal war of 1992–95, Bosnian Muslims were struggling to survive and, in the postwar period, to reconstruct their scattered life and de facto partitioned homeland. This was not a time to engage in major theoretical endeavors but rather to find simple answers to the issues of daily life.

In what follows, I present, in the fragmentary form of excerpts from interviews or debates, different views from three selected Bosnian Muslim scholars. Despite the shortcomings of this method, it can provide an insight into the main tendencies and the frame of reference of these scholars.

Alija Izetbegovic, intellectual and political leader of Bosnian Muslims.
On democracy

Very few words have been the subject of so much controversial understanding, and abuse, as the word *democracy*. I think that only the word
religion has had a similar fate throughout history. Absolute rulers rarely
admitted that they were dictators; they called themselves democrats and
asked others to consider and call them as such. Due to these controver-
sies, the United Nations, as far as I remember, published *Demokratija u
svijetu zategnutosti* which very vividly demonstrates this global misunder-
standing of democracy.

Maybe because of that, it is necessary for me to give my own opinion
on the question. I believe that God created people free and equal, that
higher or lower races do not exist, and there are neither good [n]or bad
nations. I believe that people bring with themselves a certain number of
inalienable rights, and that governments have no right to limit these rights,
much as I do not believe in the unrestricted rights of the majority, as a
tyranny of the majority is a tyranny like all others. I believe that the measure of liberty is the relationship to minorities, and that freedom of
thought is, above all, the freedom to think differently. These, in short,
constitute my understanding of democracy.[8]

Fikret Karcic, professor of Islamic law.

Marko Orsolic: I have one question which I would pose to Professor
Fikret Karcic. If there were in Bosnia and Herzegovina more than fifty
percent Muslims out of the whole population, would it be required by
Islam, by Shari'a, by Islamic law, to establish an Islamic Republic of Bosnia
and Herzegovina[?] Let me state my position: if there were in Bosnia
99.9% Catholics, I would not be in favor of a Catholic state, in fact I
would be the first to be against it!

Fikret Karcic: I believe that there are many others who could answer
this, but I will try to give my answer to this. I would start the answer by
going back to 1258 when the Mongol commander Hulaghu han destroyed
Baghdad and overthrew the caliphate. He posed a similar question to the
Baghdad ulama of the famous Nizamiyye school. Hulaghu asked: "Who
has the greater right to rule and be obeyed as a ruler—a just non-Muslim
or an unjust Muslim?" The Baghdad *ulama* replied: "A just non-Muslim."
In this religious opinion (*fatwā*), the attribute of justice is given preference
over the attribute of religion. By referring to this event several centuries
ago, I can now offer an answer to the question posed. The issue is what

meaning or social function should Islam have in Bosnia and Herzegovina, or in Yugoslavia. Whenever discussing this issue, it is important to take into account where and in what conditions this question is posed. Rosenthal in one of his books, *Islam in the Modern Nation State,* points out that the definition of Islam in the Indian sub-continent depended on where the answer came from—on one side, India, or on the other side, Pakistan.

The question and the answer are shaped by social and historical circumstances. Muslims in these areas, from the end of Turkish rule in 1878 practically and from 1908 legally, accepted that Islam be treated equally as the other religions. Such was the case in the Kingdom of Serbs, Croats, Slovenes and in the Kingdom of Yugoslavia from 1918 until 1941. Such a legally equal treatment of Islam was continued in the secular socialist state from 1946. The Islamic community accepted the separation of religious communities from the state, abolition of the Shari'a courts, and the Shari'a law in the civil sphere. As such the Islamic community accepted the definition of Islam as a religion. Hence, I think that the idea of some "Islamic republic" in Bosnia and Herzegovina falls into the domain of political fantasy or speculation. Personally I think that the secular, the truly secular model, is the most appropriate for multi-religious societies. I have doubts regarding any ideological state, and I believe that the rule of law and the manifestation of religion is defined by law, and not by political opportunism. This is the frame which is necessary for the exercise of human rights and freedoms, of which religious rights and freedoms are a part.[9]

Dzemaludin Latic, poet, professor of Qur'ānic exegesis, and political activist.

That is what I call "religious Bosnia," Bosnia "without the oppressor and the oppressed," as our Prophet (s.a.w.s.) would say.

Q: What kind of Bosnia is that? A "theocratic state"?

A: No, not a theocratic state! That would be a state where religious values are respected most, to such an extent that all four of our religious communities are a social value, and atheism is a private matter of the individual, but not a social value! In such a state, religious officials would have a say regarding drafts of laws that are before our parliament. In such a way, we would build peace among the nations of Bosnia.

Q: What do you expect from the SDA (Democratic Action Party)? What kind of SDA?

A: I would like that, not only the SDA but all Bosniak political activists and organizations, stick to the principles of Islamic politics.

Q: What principles are those?

A: I translate and publish books on this topic, but in short they are: understanding politics as a trust (*amāna*) from God; avoiding self-candidature; a humble life; distancing one's family from power without injustice to the family. The SDA should share the social crisis of its people, rather than SDA MPs receiving a salary of 3000KM. One leader should not be given all or most authority. One should never be without a leader who has religious credentials and abilities. One should not cheat ("Who cheats is not one of us"); tell the truth to enemies; have trust in those with whom you rule and achieve the trust of fellow associates; allow freedom of thought; respect the opposition, and not accuse the opposition of *coup d'état* when it is better than us; reach decisions by convincing and not by intrigues and force. Specifically, apart from the struggle for Bosnia and for the freedom of Islam in Bosnia, I expect the SDA to have a policy which I term "politics of the Bosniac whole" (*politika bosnjacke cijeline*).[10]

These three fragments show us the diversity that exists in contemporary Muslim thought in Bosnia and Herzegovina: from reference to the views of the school of natural law, through the refusal of an ideological state, to a kind of positive attitude of the state toward religious values. Within these coordinates, contemporary Muslim thought in Bosnia and Herzegovina continues to develop.

Muslim and Christian Perspectives on Different Models of Governance and Justice

၄၅

Vladimir Ciric

In most of the analyses to be found nowadays, Christianity is defined as a strict part of Western civilization and Islam as a strict part of Eastern civilization. Whether intentionally or not, these analyses always forget the fact that there are Christians—Eastern ones—who live and develop in the same civilizations and historical circumstances as Muslims do. Eastern Christians such as Greek Orthodox, Coptic Orthodox, Nestorians, and others used to live, or still do live, as a minority or majority along with Muslims, and mutual influences are present to this very day. If we take a look back, we will discover that in the times of the establishment of the Umayyad caliphate, Eastern Christians lived on the same soil; at the peak of the 'Abbāsid state, Nestorians lived alongside the other Christian churches, which enjoyed the very same privileged position. Then, in the Ottoman Empire, all Greek Orthodox patriarchates were gathered in one state, and, until the collapse of that empire, in the Balkans and Greater Syria, Eastern Christians were in an absolute majority as well. The Eastern Christian states of medieval times—Byzantium, Serbia, Bulgaria—had the same "nomocratic" system of law and governance as the Ottomans, and previously the Umayyads and 'Abbāsid, which remain today in all Islamic states.

Conversely, the Eastern Christian churches, along with the Muslims, had the same bitter experience in encounters with the crusaders, who came from the West (in all its forms) and who established a Latin Kingdom in Constantinople that lasted for seventy years. Up until recent times, the political situation in Muslim countries coincided with political climates affected by the development of nationalism in countries where the majority of the population are Greek Orthodox; the Iranian revolution turned into the defense of the nation

97

as, in the end, Khomeini affirmed state interests above Islamic ones; in Turkey, the Refah Party was more of a Turkish nationalist party with an Islamic domestic agenda. Meanwhile, Bulgaria expelled several thousand Turks and others who did not want to accept changing their surnames with the Bulgarian common suffix "-ov" and who refused to be called Bulgarians, and so the question of Bulgarian national integrity was raised; in the former Yugoslavia, the movement MASPOK claimed for Croatians a bigger influence on the society, and the memoranda of the Serbian Academy of Science and Arts raised the same questions as those raised by the Bulgarians, this time with dreadful consequences. All this points to the same civilization and historical environment in Eastern Christianity and Islam. What is it that distinguishes this Eastern civilization?

The Eastern conception of life, which is incorporated in religious teachings, is based on personalism rather than on a system of law and wide legislation. According to Orthodox teachings, it is only with a second person that we can establish communion and community. In a deeper meaning, it is in the other person that we should search for, and find, Christ. Wherever love exists, one person would always find justification and the perfection of the other, finding and discovering in this other the personality of God, the face of God, and the truth and truthful presence of God. In Islam, we may find a similar approach to the subject, recalling T. E. Lawrence's observation that "Arabs believe in individuals, not institutions."

Generally speaking, this means that personal relationships are above legal ones and are based on complete trust in the morality of the trustee. This strongly rooted personalistic point of view to a life created the title—if we may consider it a title—"neighbor." On the street or in the supermarket, an unknown person is a "neighbor." In the Balkans, as well as in Turkey and the Middle East, the neighbor and the nearest neighborhood is treated as close family, to the level of holiness. Thus Eastern Christians and Muslims have a rather strong and close-linked community. This "neighborly way of life" opens wide a door for corruption. On the one hand, this could not be strictly called corruption, because the neighbor is the one from whom one would expect to find a friend or cousin at a given institution, who could help in avoiding bureaucracy; on the other hand, this kind of help usually neglects the protection ensured by good governance of a given institution. Therefore institutions can easily fail to be just and well governed. Fortunately this corruption—if we talk about giving a bribe—is not too common a custom. Whether the bribe is defined as giving a reward in advance for a job or task that has to be finished successfully, in Eastern countries a reward is given after bringing the task to its end. There are numerous examples of thankful patients who give a reward to doctors for good treatment. Also the rewards could be given, for example, to avoid long delays in issuing driving licenses. Guided by the quotation that "a friend of my friend is a friend of mine," people in the East are prone to the custom of rewarding institutional employees, because rewarding in advance could be considered an offence.

The personalistic lifestyle has created a special taste in the East for autocracy. The figure of the president is a recognized incorporation of justice, nation, and faith, keeping leadership by fostering all together—in one word, a figure of the father—and Easterners have believed in their leaders as one believes in his father. The figure of the sovereign is the archetype of Byzantine emperors, who had all these attributes. The most common epithet for the communist sovereigns was "father of the nation," meaning that they kept nation and faith interests, and they were always those to whom the last word was given: they were considered the absolute keepers of justice. The Byzantine state system (based on nomocanons) and government had been adopted by the Umayyads from the southeast borders of the Byzantine Empire, in medieval kingdoms in the Balkans up to the late nineteenth century, and by the Ottoman Empire too, and—in various forms—it also remained in the times of communism in the Balkans.

Unfortunately, these sovereigns were, and are, prone to abuse their power and constitutionally given authorities. In multiethnic and multiconfessional countries, as Yugoslavia and the Soviet Union were, the sovereign's principle of keeping the nation together was based on the idea of "fraternity-unity." Whoever spoke against this principle was seen as a public enemy and necessarily became a political prisoner. The idea of political captivity is as old as Byzantium; in the Byzantine Empire and in the countries that were established on the Byzantine model, political prisoners and public enemies were those who were against the sovereign, or in the Middle Ages against the state religion. Speaking against religion was in the period of communism modified to speaking against the nation. The least that these "enemies" could expect was to be expelled from the soil of a particular empire or kingdom. In more recent times, expulsion for political reasons is not the method, because of the institution of asylum. Thus in the West there are many asylum seekers from Eastern countries who were directly faced with repressive regimes in their native countries. For example, Slobodan Milosevic's regime insisted on keeping the Serbian national and religious identity above others, completely neglecting and denying other identities and their impact on Serbian identity. So this regime exerted tyranny on all outside the Serbian identity, including national, religious, cultural, and other identities. Many people emigrated then or sought asylum in order to escape the madness of this tyranny. Conversely, in the post-Milosevic era, the leadership of democrats and democratic movements has brought confusion to the people; so the Radical Party, with an ultranationalist conception, appears to be the most popular party. In Bulgaria today, the prime minister is actually heir to the throne and is expected by the Bulgarian people to pull the nation together. This shows a possible preference of Bulgarians for an "iron hand" in someone capable of leading the nation. Nationalism sows the seed of autocracy, to which all Eastern nations are very prone.

The nomocanonical law system, still present in the legislation of Muslim countries, does not exist today in the legislation of countries where a Greek Orthodox majority lives; yet some tendencies still remain and are evident. The leaderships of these countries usually ask for the opinion of the church, especially on questions of national interest, reflecting the role the church had historically and the fact that the church kept national and religious identities aligned. From the point of view of state leadership, the church is seen as an intermediary between government and people. Every idea supported by the church is always welcomed warmly among the Orthodox people, so the place and the position of the church are very significant. For example, the withdrawal of the proposed national anthem of Serbia and Montenegro took place at the insistence of the church. The Greek lobby in America always has a church representative in negotiations. In Muslim countries, too, the opinion of religious authorities is strong, and they participate in decision making in particular states. The opinion of religious authorities in the East has such a strong influence that the rejection of some human rights issues can be traced to the fact that human rights are not always in accordance with Islam or Christianity in general.

How then is it possible to overcome the unjust phenomena of corruption, autocracy, and the rejection of human rights? The pattern of repulsing corruption in Swaziland is an extremely good example. According to this, giving rewards is now allowed and has become legal, as it is considered an act of charity. Because the salaries of employees in government and medical institutions are chronically low in the Balkan countries, giving rewards for a job well done would not be considered a bribe, but an act of charity. The law would act, however, if the reward were given in advance, when it would be considered a bribe. Pyramidal responsibility can monitor institutions such as the courts in order to obtain just and fair trials. Conversely, the less corrupt the official government, the less corrupt society as a whole. As the opinions of religious authorities are very important, fruitful dialogue has to begin on the basis of a complete respect for different identities, with open communication to each other. The religious authorities should be included in making decisions in order to find the best solutions for the common good and for building a better society. In addition to including them in decision making, religious authorities can also make efforts to overcome ignorance about other faiths, because this kind of ignorance is present in both Christians and Muslims. Christians do not know much about Islam, and Muslims do not know much about Christianity. Once this ignorance is overcome, people would be more tolerant, have a better understanding of one another's needs, and be able to live in harmony.

Government and Religion in Malaysia

७๑

Mohammad Hashim Kamali

Malaysia is a majority Muslim country wherein Islam is the official religion but where non-Muslims also enjoy freedom of religion and worship. Ethnicity and religion are probably two of the most challenging aspects of government in Malaysia, and there is always room for improvement, due partly to changing perceptions of inter faith relations among the Muslims and non-Muslims of Malaysia, the impact of Islamic revivalism, and the changing expectations of civil society of all faiths as to the role and attitude of the government concerning religion. Engagement over details in inter faith relations hardly fails to be contentious and can easily lead to differences of opinion, but this is not the main purpose of this study, which is to provide a panoramic view of government and religion in Malaysia.

Notwithstanding my own reservations and criticism over detailed issues, I propose not to engage the reader in details but to offer a general view, which I begin with a leading statement that Malaysia's overall record on the subject of our concern is, on the whole, positive. Among the Muslim countries Malaysia has often been cited as a good example of a pluralist society that has nurtured accommodation and tolerance of different religions and cultures. The government has taken measures to provide space and opportunity for participation in almost every walk of life for its non-Muslim citizens. Religious and cultural pluralism is a basic framework and criterion of decision making and a policy theme of almost every national leader, including the current prime minister, Abdullah Badawi, who made a landmark policy statement on Islam in the 55th General Assembly of the ruling party, the United Malay National Organisation (UMNO) in September 2004. Abdullah Badawi introduced a fresh understanding of Islam under the rubric of *Islām Hadhāri*, or "civilizational Islam." He did this following his landslide election victory in the March 2004 elections. The precise definition and understanding of *Islām Hadhārī* has been the focus of media attention ever since, and even though the coalition government that consists mainly of the Malay, Chinese, and Indian component parties have adopted *Islām Hadhārī* in their election manifesto, many have remained skeptical about the wider implications thereof. The concept has stimulated extensive civil society discourse and engagement in the detailed analysis of this theme. It is not my purpose here to discuss details but merely to underscore the changes Malaysia is experiencing in its policy formulations concerning Islam and other religions. In his maiden speech on the subject, the prime minister laid stress on the broader civilizational appeal of Islam to Malaysians of all faiths and spelled out a ten-point scheme that constitutes the basic themes and engagements of *Islām Hadhārī*. These are (a) faith and piety in Allah, (b) a just and trustworthy government, (c) a free and independent people, (d) mastery of knowledge, (e) balanced and comprehensive economic developments, (f) a good quality of life, (g) protection of the rights of minority groups and women, (h) cultural and moral integrity, (i) safeguarding the environment, and (j) strong defense capabilities.

The prime minister explained that these principles have been formulated to ensure that their implementation and approach do not cause anxiety among any group in our multiracial and multireligious country. They are also meant to empower Muslims to face the global challenges of today. The prime minister characterized *Islām Hadhārī* as "an approach that emphasises development, consistent with the tenets of Islam, and focuses on enhancing the quality of life." This is to be achieved, he added, via the mastery of knowledge and the development of the nation; the implementation of a dynamic economic, trading, and financial system; and integrated and balanced development that creates a knowledgeable and pious people who hold noble values and are honest, trustworthy, and prepared to take on global challenges.

Islām Hadhārī basically implies an engagement in the broader and universal values and principles of Islam that contemplates the presence of human communities next to their neighbors and outsiders. The usage in the prime minister's speech of "*Islām Hadhārī*" instead of the more familiar term "*Hadhārah Islām*" or "*Hadhārah Islāmiyyah*" ("Islamic civilization") is, I believe, intended to imply a certain focus on the broader values of Islam of relevance to Malaysia as it is at present and not so much as it was in historical times. It is also concerned with Islamic values of interest and relevance to other civiliza-tions, religions, and cultures. The term may also be said to be suggestive of a positive response to the cultural dimension of globalization that is more closely akin to the value structure of Western civilization and its scientific and techno-logical achievements. It is expressive of the concern as to how Muslims can have a constructive engagement with modernity, people's well-being, and a democratic and welfare-oriented government. Since *Hadhārah Islāmiyyah* (Islamic civilization) was seen to be more focused on historical Islam, which now stands in a different set of relationships from the supremacy it once enjoyed in earlier times, the new expression seeks to focus on the present struc-ture of values and relationships with modernity as well as a progressive outlook on prosperity and economic development.

Religious pluralism in Malaysia is manifested by the fact that its popula-tion of 26 million is composed of about 14 million (or 55%) Malay Muslims, although there are also Muslims of Indian and Chinese descent that raise the total component of Muslims to 58.6 percent. Non-Muslims constitute about 40 percent of the population consisting of Buddhists (19%), Christians (8.1%), Hindus (6.4%), and Confucians and others (5.3%). Members of the indigenous tribes of Sabah and Sarawak and aboriginals of West Malaysia have animistic beliefs, although many Dayaks, Ibans, and Kadazans of East Malaysia have converted to Catholicism.

The Christian community is presently the fastest growing religious minority in Malaysia. In 1921 they comprised a mere 1.7 percent of the popula-tion, and they had, by 1980, grown to 6.4 percent. Just ten years later, 8.1 percent of the population identified themselves as Christians. Although Chris-tians still constitute a relatively small segment of the population in most states, in Sabah and Sarawak they account for 27 percent and 37 percent, respectively. Almost 80 percent of Christians in Malaysia are Catholics, with Protestants accounting for the balance. Christianity in Malaysia has steadily grown among urban Indians, Chinese, and Eurasians.

Religious pluralism is basically not conducive to harmony. Multireligious societies like Malaysia and Lebanon have experienced difficulties on their path to nation building. Yet if seen positively, religious and cultural pluralism can be a source of enrichment and a character-building influence for individuals and communities.

Every one of the major religious traditions that have followers in Malaysia encourages justice and tolerance in their dealings with other religions and communities. Virtually all of them subscribe to what is known as the Golden Rule that represents the common goal and motto of the Malaysian Interfaith Network, namely to "treat others as you would like to be treated."[11] Buddhism teaches that "you treat all creatures as you would like to be treated." Hinduism puts it as "not doing to others that which if done to you would cause pain." Christianity has similarly emphasized the spirit of "love thy neighbor," charity, and compassion. The basic ideals of justice and moral virtue, the criteria of right and wrong, and cooperation in pursuit of good values in Christianity closely resemble those of their Islamic counterparts. The Qur'ān has in more than one place declared itself as an affirmation of the values contained in the Bible and the Torah.

The Prophet Muhammad declared love for one's brother and neighbor as an integral part of the Muslim faith. The Qur'ān emphasized the fraternity of humankind (*al-Baqara* 2:213; *al-Nisā'* 4:1), commitment to universal justice (*al-Nisā'* 4:58; *al-Māi'da* 5:8; *al-Mumtaḥana* 60:80), promotion of good and prevention of evil (*Āl 'Imrān* 3:104, 110; *al-Ḥajj* 22:41), acceptance of religious diversity (*al-Ḥajj* 22:67; *al-Baqara* 2:256; *al-Kāfirūn* 109:6), and recognition of moral virtue as the only marks of distinction for individuals and nations (*al-Ḥujurāt* 49:13). The Malays' outlook is influenced by these teachings and by their own history of having experienced the somewhat belated entry into Islam (as of the fourteenth century CE) through the peaceful influences of traders, Sufi saints, and the benign royal patronage of the early Sultanates in the region. The fact that Malaysia was geographically a stage away from the mainstay of the Middle Eastern military arena also contributed to the relatively tolerant disposition of its people and their corresponding international image.

Religion in the Constitution

Article 3 of the Federal Constitution of 1957 provides that "Islam shall be the religion of the Federation, but other religions may be practised in peace and harmony in any part of the Federation." Article 11 provides that every person has the right to profess and practice his religion and also to propagate it— subject to restrictions that may be determined by law. Every religious group has the right to manage its own affairs, to establish and maintain institutions for charitable purposes, and to acquire property. Article 12 authorizes the government "to establish or maintain Islamic institutions" that provide instruction in Islam and incur such expenditure as may be necessary for that purpose. Many state-aided Islamic institutions, such as Pusat Islam, the International Islamic University Malaysia, Institute of Islamic Understanding Malaysia, the *hajj* organization (Tabung Haji), and so forth, have been established as a result. No person is required to receive instruction or take part in any ceremony or act of worship of a religion other than his own. Part two of the constitution, which spells out these and other fundamental rights and liberties—such as equality before the law and freedom of speech, movement, assembly, and association as well as the rights to property and ownership—is applicable to all citizens regardless of ethnicity and creed.[12]

The Malay Rulers (Sultans), who are the heads of religion in their respective states, are required by the state constitutions to be Muslims. Initially most of these constitutions required leading state officials, including the chief minister and state secretary, also to be Muslims. After independence, however, some of these provisions were amended to enable a ruler to appoint a non-Muslim chief minister who enjoys majority support in the state legislature. There is nothing in the federal constitution, however, requiring the prime minister or any minister or official of the federal government to be a Muslim.

Although Islam is the religion of the federation, there is no head of the Muslim religion for the whole of the federation. The king (Yang di-Pertuan Agong) continues to be the head of religion in his own state and in the Federal Territory, Melaka, Penang, Sabah, and Sarawak, as these states have no Malay rulers of their own. The king's representatives in these states, known as Yang di-Pertuan Negeri, are effectively the patrons of religion.

Malaysian leaders and judges have often discussed the implications of article 3 on the character of the country and government and have generally maintained that it is confined to ceremonial matters. State ceremonies such as recitation of Islamic prayers (*do'a*) at the opening and closing of official government functions, the installation or the birthday of the king, and Independence Day are thus conducted in accordance with Islamic rituals.

In the early 1950s, it was not yet determined whether the non-Malay and non-Muslim inhabitants of the peninsula would be granted citizenship. The UMNO and the Malay Chinese Association (MCA) reached an agreement that the Chinese would accept declaration of Islam as the state religion and Malay as the official language of the federation. The Malays for their part agreed that non-Malays born in the country after independence should automatically become Malaysian citizens. As part of this "bargain," certain privileges were also granted to the Malays pertaining to land ownership under article 89 of the constitution and the application of quotas in favor of the Malays and natives in public services, scholarships, and business licenses.[13] These provisions are sometimes seen as preferential and discriminatory by non-Malays. In practice the government has applied policies that seek to establish a certain balance in the participation levels of the various strata of the population in the economy and government.

Non-Muslims have often voiced concern over issues pertaining to equality before the law, matters relating to conversion, especially of persons below the age of majority, and inter faith relations; they have acknowledged in the meantime that some issues have received attention, although unresolved issues have also been noted. Most commentators would not underestimate the challenge of finding more refined solutions to outstanding issues, yet the positive side of the picture and the willingness to make further improvement have on the whole remained the more dominant.

Since its establishment in 1983, the Malaysian Consultative Council of Buddhism, Christianity, Hinduism and Sikhism (MCCBCHS) has served as an umbrella organization for non-Muslims to convey their views to government agencies on such matters as the establishment of new places of worship, invitation of visitors and priests from overseas, and AIDS and drug-related issues. The allocation of land for the building of churches, temples, and cemeteries has also been discussed. In a 1983 conference of chief ministers of Malaysia, it was agreed to control the somewhat indiscriminate building of shrines, churches, and temples. The prime minister, Dr. Mahathir, in a 1994 speech, confirmed this and noted, "If you look at Kuala Lumpur, you see churches and temples, and sometimes more churches than mosques, but we are not concerned about that." But if one puts up a church in a community that is 90 percent Muslim, it may not be well received. It would be equally unwelcome to "build a mosque in the middle of a Hindu community." The MCCBCHS does not receive any direct funding from the government, yet the prime minister and other dignitaries have often participated in their fund-raising activities. It has been suggested that a non-Muslim affairs department of government should be established to address minority religious matters on a more regular basis.

Religious minorities in Malaysia are able, on the whole, to practice their own forms of worship, religious holidays, and festivals and to maintain religious organizations and their own schools. There is a tendency toward isolation, as the religious groups are inclined to live in separate localities, to establish and maintain separate schools and institutions, to publish separate newspapers and the like, yet there has been no real fragmentation of the society. The Islamic revivalist movement of recent decades has also had the effect, to some extent, on other religious groups to accentuate their own ethnoreligious identities and revivalisms, as it were, of their own. Yet the various groups have respected each other's differences and even contributed positively to the cultural diversity of Malaysia.

Most of the public holidays of Malaysia, such as Aidil Fitri, Christmas, Wesak (Buddhist), Deepavali (Hindu), and the Chinese New Year, have some religious signification. The Malay Open House tradition of Aidil Fitri, which has also been adopted by the Chinese and Indians of Malaysia, serves a good purpose in encouraging social interaction across the ethnoreligious divides. The five festivals mentioned are all observed as national holidays, whereas Thaipusam is observed as an additional Hindu holiday in five states of Malaysia. Good Friday is a public holiday in Sabah and Sarawak where Christians represent sizable segments of the population. It is customary for leading figures and personalities in the government and other community leaders, friends, and associates to visit their open houses and visit each other on personal occasions such as weddings, birthdays, hospitalizations, and funerals.

Religious minorities have occasionally expressed concern over the disproportionate time allocation in the electronic media to Islamic and other religious programs. The MCCBCHS has noted that very little air time—and only during festive seasons—is given to non-Muslim religions. The call to prayer (*adhān*) heard over the radio and other Islamic programs in the media are obviously not matched by equivalent input from other religions. This may to some extent be a consequence of Islam's being the official religion of Malaysia. Yet Malaysian television is multilingual, offering a variety of programs from local sources (American, Chinese, Indian, etc.) almost regardless of religious considerations. Pious Muslims are also critical of television programs saturated by Western productions that tend to cultivate attitudes insensitive to Islamic teachings. Yet the Malaysian broadsheet and electronic media do, on the whole, convey openness and regard for the sensitivities of a multireligious audience.

Non-Muslim Participation in Public Life

In line with the pluralistic character of Malaysia, the government has underscored the need for all groups to work together and has devised policies that emphasize harmony among Muslims and non-Muslims. About one-third or more of the Malaysian members of Parliament are non-Muslim and non-Malay. This is also true of the federal cabinet and other government organizations. The non-Muslim ministers tend to play a key role in voicing the concerns of their respective ethnoreligious communities. In his renowned 1996 Oxford lecture "Islam, the Misunderstood Religion," Prime Minister Dr. Mahathir stated, "Although the Muslims have a sufficient majority to rule the country on their own, they have chosen not to do so. Instead they deliberately chose to share power with the non-Muslim minorities."[14] In Sabah and Sarawak, which have sizable Christian and Buddhist minorities, the federal government applies the policy that the post of chief minister of the state should rotate between the three religious groups (Muslims, Christians, and Buddhists) of those states.

The New Economic Policy (NEP) that was implemented between 1971 and 1990 had as its first goal the eradication of poverty for all citizens but also paid some attention to minimizing economic disparities between Muslims and non-Muslims. Poverty is widespread among the Malays, and the fact that business and industry and much of the wealth are concentrated among the Chinese and Indians had become a bone of contention that the government had to address. This is counterbalanced to some extent by the fact that the Malays are more dominant in the government. The NEP projected an increase in the intake of Malay students in institutions of higher learning; the government followed this but also maintained an ethnoreligious balance of limiting Malay and native recruitment to 55 percent of the total.

The National Development Policy (NDP), which followed the NEP for another ten years (1990–2000), continued the policy of giving greater assistance to the Malays; it was hoped that by the close of the century economic disparities between the Malays and non-Malays would be largely eliminated. The NDP achieved most of its goals, but the target of 30 percent control of corporate wealth by the Malays was not achieved, although the Malay portion rose from 1 percent in 1970 to 19.1 percent in 1999. Government leaders have in the meantime expressed the desire that everyone should eventually participate on the basis of qualification and merit regardless of ethnicity and religion.

Participation in civil society associations is on the whole nondenominational. Membership of associations, such as environmental groups, consumer groups, human rights groups, and women's groups, include people from all religions. All faith communities also have their own denominational groups and associations that maintain generally a lively and varied agenda of activities. They are mostly independent of government, although some receive financial support if their line of activity happens to be proactive to the government's own policy and program.

In the sphere of education, Malaysia has retained its traditional Islamic religious schools and madrasahs, some of which have been upgraded in recent years, and many are recipients of financial support from the government. There are also numerous international, Chinese, and Indian schools in Malaysia that offer study programs in their respective languages and religions; many are successful and often a preferred choice compared with the government schools.

Government schools are open to all Malaysians, and no discrimination is noted on grounds of ethnicity and religion in admission to these schools. A certain complaint has, however, been voiced that non-Muslims cannot provide religious instruction for their children in government schools, in contrast to the provision of such instruction to Muslim children. It has been suggested that while Muslims are attending their Islamic religious classes, other religious communities should be permitted to teach their own religions during this time.

With the exception of perhaps Christians, who tend to receive outside support, and also the Chinese, whose schools enjoy good patronage within Malaysia, the other religious minorities have noted a certain shortage of qualified religious teachers and personnel, which is due partly to lack of direct government funding and also due to restrictions on the number of invited religious teachers and speakers from abroad. Minority religious groups have also spoken of the difficulty they have faced in securing permission and land to build churches and temples. Thus they say that developers are normally required to include community mosques in their plans, but no such allocation is made for temples and churches. Non-Muslim representative speakers have stated, nevertheless, that the government does allocate land, if its requirements are met and when proper procedures are followed.

The Application of Islamic Law

The application of Islamic law in Malaysia is confined to Muslims, and even among Muslims it is limited to matters of personal status, such as matrimonial law, worship matters, religious charities, inheritance, and bequest. The detailed list of subjects and jurisdiction over them is regulated in the three lists that appear under the ninth schedule of the constitution—namely, the state list, the federal list, and the concurrent list. This is also a restrictive approach in that the wider areas of Islamic law falling outside the scope of these lists are not enforceable in Malaysia. The definition of law in the constitution does not include Islamic law.[15] Article 4 identifies the constitution as the supreme law of the federation, and any law that is inconsistent with it "shall to the extent of inconsistency be void."

Islamic law in Malaysia is basically a state matter that falls within the jurisdiction of each state. Hence Parliament cannot make law dealing with Syariah matters except for the federal territories of Kuala Lumpur and Labuan. Typically each state has laws usually called the "Administration of Islamic Law Enactment," setting up the state's Islamic Religious Council and the Syariah courts and also articulating religious offences and their penalties. However, the state list specifically provides that the regulatory powers of the states on Islamic law and religion apply only to "persons professing the religion of Islam."

Since the Islamic Party of Malaysia (*Parti Islam Semalaysia*, PAS) won the 1990 election in Kelantan, it has asserted its views on the Islamic state and Syariah. A second Eastern state in the Malay belt, namely Terengganu, also elected a PAS-dominated government in the 1999 elections. Terengganu was won back by UMNO in the 2003 elections and with it the PAS also lost much ground in Parliament. But the rise of the Islamic party to prominence had caused apprehensions among the non-Muslims of Malaysia. PAS's election manifesto consistently maintained its objective of establishing an Islamic state in Malaysia. In 1993, Kelantan introduced the renowned Hudud bill, after approval by the state legislature and the sultan. Since then, PAS has also introduced other restrictive measures on women's dress and participation in the workplace, gaming, and businesses, and so on, which non-Muslims viewed with apprehension. Although the federal government has blocked the Hudud bill due to problems over jurisdiction, and PAS also lost much of its influence over the years, the issues are still the focus of public attention.

Seen more objectively, one may add that Syariah-related issues have remained contentious media and civil society topics in Malaysia that have not seriously threatened sociopolitical stability in the country. Significantly, Malaysia has held seven consecutive elections since the ethnic unrest of 1969, with the participation of opposition parties in all of them and without serious election malpractices. If there are tensions over divisive issues, they have been generally contained under both the Barisan (national front) government and their counterparts in Kelantan and Terengganu.

Conclusion

Malaysia's economic success in recent decades and its relative economic prosperity have been contributing factors to peaceful ethnoreligious relations among its various religious groups. With almost full employment of the available labor force, people are engaged in industries and professions in both the government and private sectors, and they obviously favor continuity. Religious and sectarian differences are contained, and people are able to maintain a certain perspective over issues. Yet the sources of tension are long term and can easily be provoked with relatively minor incidents. Ethnicity and religion are thus likely to take a high profile in Malaysian politics for the foreseeable future. These are enduring policy issues, and further adjustment in national planning to ascertain greater objectivity and equilibrium in intercommunity relations would be expected, and indeed desirable. Economic success has also placed the government in a stronger position now to take more definite steps in that direction, and the signs are that this will be the likely trend under the current prime minister, who has frequently spoken in support of harmonious relations among the Muslims and non-Muslims of Malaysia. His new policy engagement in *Islām Hadhārī* obviously contemplates a fresh projection of the teachings of Islam of relevance to contemporary concerns. Its focus on people's welfare and a service-oriented government augurs well for the future of unity among the various strata of Malaysian society.

of the nation-state system. In a recent poll by a private radio station, JOY FM in Ghana, 85 percent of Ghanaians said they did not see any reason to die for their country. Hence the whole idea of the nation-state in West Africa is frequently questioned and in some cases openly rejected.

Debates over Systems of Governance and Justice

After independence, the colonial powers handed over to Africans a nation-state system that they (the colonialists) had not attempted to run themselves. The British, for instance, did not govern their colonies such as Gold Coast, Nigeria, or Sudan as single, unitary states. In all these countries, the Muslim North and Christian/Animist South related to the colonial authorities under different political and judicial arrangements. These communities therefore had little direct contact and relationship with each other in the political sphere. In addition, even though the colonialists practiced multiparty democracies back in their home countries, multiparty democracy was, for whatever reason, not implemented in the new nation-states. When Africans were handed this strange animal called "nation-state," the risk that the different regional, ethnic, and religious groups would go their own ways was real. Separatist movements in Ghana and Nigeria erupted into open conflict during the Biafra war in the mid-1960s. Under such circumstances dissent was viewed as dangerous, and—in a bid to enforce national unity—the dictatorial one-party system of governance became the norm.

The persistent dissent and refusal to accept the new nation-state concept on the one hand, and the suppression and oppression that in most cases accompanied the one-party systems on the other hand, fueled more violent secessionist and rebellious campaigns as well as military coups that bedeviled most African nations from the mid-1960s until the early 1990s. After the collapse of communism, pressure from Western governments and from internal oppositions began to mount on military dictatorships in Africa, all agitating for Western-style multiparty democracy. Under these pressures countries such as Liberia, Sierra Leone, and later Cote D'Ivoire erupted into civil war. These times also coincided with the global resurgence of Islam and Muslim awareness. With the discovery of oil, the Muslim Middle East became an important player on the African scene. African Muslims in countries such as Sudan and Nigeria started agitating for the

Shari'a system of governance as an alternative to secular multiparty democracy. All-out civil war broke out in the Sudan while sporadic violence became part of the northern Nigerian body polity. From this time on, debate in countries with significant Muslim populations became what some have called "shariacracy" (adoption of Islamic law as the basis of governance and its expansion into the criminal justice system) versus Western-style democracy.[16]

The Muslim Case

African Muslims who are suspicious of and/or reject secular democracy do so for various reasons. Ali Mazrui, a leading African Muslim intellectual, writes that secularism is "the greatest threat" to the advancement of Islam in Africa.[17] This threat, as far as some are concerned, was deliberately imposed on Muslim Africa to undermine the implementation of the Shari'a. Ibraheem Sulaiman, of the Ahmadu Bello University in Nigeria, writes of the British colonial power's waging "war on the Shari'a" with the view of ensuring "the eventual ascendancy of secularisation in Nigeria, at all costs."[18] In effect, therefore, secular democracy is seen as a threat to the Islamic way of life and should be opposed. In addition to the conspiracy theories, according to which secular democracy seeks to undermine the Shari'a, Muslim objections have to do with the fact that secular democracy is founded upon the sixteenth-century West European Enlightenment and a legacy of Western Christian heritage. Ibraheem Sulaiman, writing earlier on the subject, noted: "To the extent that secularism was imposed on the people by the same power that imposed Christianity, the two approaches to life can logically be construed as representing the two faces of the same coin: Western Imperialism. Muslims have therefore no reason to accept secular values, or to have any faith in secularism."[19] Writing on what he calls the "Hidden Christian Agenda," Ali Mazrui declares that "the concept of the secular state is itself Christian. That is the most ironic part of it all."[20] The "Christian" and Western roots or connections with secular democracy are therefore another source of concern to Muslims. The adoption or implementation of Shari'a in the Nigerian context is seen as a way that northern Nigerian Muslims are trying to assert their cultural identity in contradistinction to their Christian southern counterparts and thereby to insulate themselves from the effects of globalization and westernization.[21] Isma'il al-Faruqi, though not an

African Muslim, once lamented in the context of a discussion of appropriate systems of governance in Africa and Asia, that "it is a real pity that Asians and Africans should yearn after the kind of state which was born out of the intellectual and spiritual movements in Europe beginning with the Reformation and finishing in the nineteenth century Romanticism."[22]

Like the eighteenth- and nineteenth-century West African jihadists who renounced the sociopolitical institutions of their time, contemporary Muslim revivalists regard Western-inspired democratic pluralism, which essentially involves choice, as *kufr*. But the Muslim concern is much more profound. For instance, secular democracy, which operates on the principle of separation of church and state, is seen to have its roots in Christianity. Jesus's saying "Render therefore to Caesar the things that are Caesar's, and to God the things that are God's" is held (rightly or wrongly) to be the main inspiration for the notion of separation between the spiritual and temporal (Matt. 22:21). Muslims, conversely, have a completely different model in the experience of Muhammad, who in Medina was not just a religious leader but a soldier and a statesman. The system of governance that Muhammad inaugurated in Medina between 622 and 632, where spiritual and temporal were fused together, is held by Muslims to be the divinely sanctioned and only acceptable system of governance for them for all time. To quote Sulaiman: "This is the eternal, unalterable model—the Sunna—laid down by the blessed Prophet for all times, and for mankind. It is, moreover, the only acceptable framework for Muslims. Muslims have, therefore, an eternal obligation not merely to live as a religious community, but to set up for themselves a state which will safeguard the interests of all people and enhance their moral integrity; a state where Islamic ideals can be given concrete manifestation."[23]

Apart from the previously mentioned concerns, Muslims also feel strongly that the Shari'a is about rediscovering and reinstating their "glorious past" overthrown by Western colonial intervention and the imposition of secular democracy. At an Islamic conference in Abuja, Nigeria, in 1989, scores of African Muslim scholars and activists decried Western cultural and ideological influences and in a resolution lamented Africa's predicament as "the object of imperial plunder and serving as a theatre for Europeans to fight proxy wars" and "of being a dumping ground for cultural and ideological ideas." The participants resolved to "encourage the teaching of Arabic . . . as the lingua franca of the continent" and to "struggle to re-instate the application of the Shari'a."[24] Out of this conference, the *Islam in Africa Organisation* was set up. Part of the preamble to the charter of the organization speaks of the participants' "being determined to sustain the momentum of global Islamic resurgence and further encourage co-operation, understanding and the brotherhood of the Umma; and desirous of forging a common front to unite the Umma with the view of facing the common enemies—the imperialist and Zionist forces of domination and secularisation, illiteracy, poverty and degradation—*and to rediscover and reinstate Africa's glorious Islamic past.*"[25] The "glorious Islamic past" here refers to the nineteenth-century jihadist rule of parts of West Africa. A key part of this rediscovery process is to seek the implementation of the Shari'a, which, as discussed earlier, was in Muslim opinion deliberately undermined by the colonial powers. Hence the international conference on Shari'a held in the United Kingdom in April 2001 discussed the "restoration" of the Shari'a in Nigeria.[26] The Shari'a in its totality to Muslims, therefore, is not just a legal, sociopolitical, and economic code but an integral part of their history and, as such, of their identity. On this basis, Muslims contend that Shari'a is about freedom of religion: It is an integral part of their faith that cannot be compromised. Making the point of freedom of religion as enshrined in the Nigerian constitution, Auwalu Hamisu Yadudu of Nigeria observes:

> Firstly, section 38 of the 1999 constitution guarantees freedom of religion. A Muslim firmly believes that his submission to the Will of Allah is inchoate if he were to choose or be made to follow some part of His, Allah's, injunctions, the personal law, and abandon others, the penal system. The Shari'a, defined as the Path which embodies the totality of Islamic guidance, seeks to govern every aspect of a believer's life. Islam, being a complete way of life for the believers, knows not the dichotomy so much flaunted by non-Muslims, especially Christians, that religion is a private affair of the individual. To the best of his belief, therefore, a Muslim conceives of his faith as demanding a total submission to the Shari'a. To a Muslim, freedom of conscience and to profess a religion of his choice alone or in company of others amounts to not much if a pre-condition, which by the way may be perfectly acceptable to followers of other religions, is stipulated for him.[27]

Both in the Sudan and Nigeria, Muslims have argued that the Shari'a is enforced only in Muslim areas, the Muslim-dominated northern parts of both countries. The Shari'a has nothing to do with non-Muslims. The Christian opposition, according to Muslims, is out of ignorance of and prejudice toward

Islam in general and the Shari'a in particular. Making this point, Lamido Sanusi observes that

> the fear of Christians is understandable. They have not read the Quran and Hadith, the sources of Islamic law, and seen where Allah and His prophets explicitly enjoined Muslims to ensure that they respect the religious rights of others and to treat adherents of other faiths with kindness and justice unless they commit an aggression against Moslems on account of their faith. Christians have not been allowed to read the history of Islamic states, to know the position of Jews and Christians in the Abbasid and Ottoman Empires, for instance, and to compare this with the position of even "non-Orthodox" Christians under the system run by the Fathers.[28]

A West African Christian Perspective

It has to be said from the outset that the Christian response, or rather reaction, to the Shari'a debate has almost always been knee-jerk and defensive. As rightly pointed out by Lamin Sanneh, "The debate as it has been conducted in Nigeria has been a one-sided affair in which Muslims have taken the offensive and Christians have reacted with high-decibel slogans about pluralism and multiculturalism."[29] Much of the Christian response therefore can be said to be out of ignorance, prejudice, and misinformation. Non-Muslim ideas about the Shari'a tend to derive more from sensationalist journalism and fear of the "Islamic threat" than from any knowledge of the Islamic legal code. Rabiatu Ammah, a Ghanaian Muslim intellectual, observes that, when it comes to misinformation about the Shari'a, "Muslim attitudes have not helped the situation in several cases—for example in Nigeria, where the application of Islamisation seems to be more interested in flogging (especially of women) rather than in creating wealth."[30] In fact, Rabiatu, a Muslim herself, says that a woman is just as concerned about the way the Shari'a is being implemented. On the part of Christians, the fear basically is that the Shari'a accords Muslims a sociopolitical and religious superiority over non-Muslims and that there are numerous discriminatory edicts in the Shari'a that will relegate Christians to the status of second-class citizens.

Can Christian fears and concerns about the Shari'a be dismissed simply as misinformed and baseless? Bert F. Breiner observes that, Christian misunderstandings and prejudices notwithstanding, there are certain areas within classical formulations of Islamic law which, "even when properly understood, still seem to the Christian to constitute an intolerable infringement of human rights."[31] Some of these include the fact that in a Shari'a state non-Muslims cannot aspire to key positions that involve exercising authority over Muslims; there are restrictions on Christian worship and witness; there is no equality before the law, as Christians cannot give evidence in a Shari'a court; and so on. The Muslim argument that the Shari'a applies only to Muslims therefore does not address the Christian concerns—especially so in the West African context, where multiple religious communities live side by side and even in a single family unit. The designation of Christians as *dhimmīs*, "protected people," in Islamic law is itself offensive to Christians, who insist on equal citizenship. As far as Christians are concerned, signing on to the Shari'a as contained in the classical formulations is about signing up for their own religious and sociopolitical subjugation by Muslims.

While a Christian perspective might agree with the Muslim objections to secular democracy on the basis that it has Western, Christian roots and is therefore imperialistic, it also points out that the Shari'a has Arab-Islamic roots and is equally imperialistic. Why replace one tool of imperialism with another? Christians also point out that, if secularism is a product of Western, Christian civilization, so is the model of the nation-state that most of the world, including Africa, has now adopted. In other words, the nations we have today, such as Ghana, Nigeria, Sudan, Kenya, and South Africa, are all products of the Western, Christian dispensation. To insist on imposing Shari'a as the basis of governance, to the Christian mind, is like buying a diesel vehicle and insisting on using regular gasoline to run it. To use a Biblical dictum, it is like "putting new wine into old wineskins." The solution to the dilemma is therefore more complex than simply throwing off secular democracy and taking on Shari'a, or vice versa. The truth is that our current collective African experience is very different from the areas from which we are vying and fighting each other to import systems of governance wholesale for implementation.

What is unique about the religious plurality of Africa is that—unlike, say, Western "Christian" Europe or most parts of North Africa and the Middle East, where the "religious other" largely corresponds to immigrant or nonindigenous communities—in Africa the "religious others" are blood relations, members of the same ethnic and linguistic units, or fully fledged fellow nationals such as Ghanaians, Nigerians, or Kenyans. The measure of any system of governance in Africa should not, therefore, necessarily be the origins of such a system but rather the ways in which it ensures equal citizenship and guarantees full representation and participation in public life in a religiously and ethnically pluralistic society. Any system that fails to take cognizance of the inherent diversity of the African context, or that seeks to treat any ethnic or religious group(s) as anything other than full nationals with equal rights and responsibilities, is bound to incite conflict. The engagement and exchanges between Africa and the West or the East in this regard therefore have to be critical. A wholesale importation of systems of governance, be it from the West or the East, will only serve to perpetuate Africa's predicament of being "the dumping ground of cultural and ideological ideas."[32]

Bert Breiner points to the issue of mistrust between Muslims and Christians as part of the problem.[33] At the heart of all the passionate discussions on both sides is the question of trust, or rather mutual mistrust. Let us assume for the sake of argument that the Shari'a is just and fair and will guarantee minority rights, as Muslims claim. There still remains the possibility of corruption and perversion by those who administer it. History is full of people who have failed to live up to the ideals they profess. Non-Muslims cannot trust Muslims not to abuse the privileged position accorded them, almost by definition, in the Shari'a. Poverty and corruption, which have become endemic in many African countries, heighten the chances of abuse and misuse of a system like the Shari'a. The mistrust is compounded in some contexts by the historical experience of non-Muslims under Islamic rule. In the northern Nigerian and Southern Sudan contexts, for instance, the period Muslims look back to as the "glorious Islamic past" only evokes on the part of non-Muslims (now largely Christians) memories of discrimination, marginalization, subordination, and slavery. These are legitimate concerns and fears that have to be taken into account in the discourse of alternative systems of governance.

Conclusion: Dilemmas and Gaps

From the foregoing discourse, it is clear that Muslims have a strong argument: first, that secular democracy has Christian roots and in essence goes against the grain of Islamic teaching. To impose secular norms and values on them is not fair. Second, that the Shari'a is an integral part of the Islamic faith, and to deny

Muslims the opportunity to observe it fully, is to deny them freedom of religion, as enshrined in the various constitutions of West African countries. These are legitimate concerns for Christians to bear in mind in the Shari'a debate. On the same note, it is equally important for Muslims not to brush aside the Christian concerns and reservations raised earlier. The truth is, as the Sudanese Muslim scholar and legal expert Abdullahi Ahmed an-Na'im points out: "There is a fundamental tension, for example, between Shari'a notions of the Muslim umma (the exclusive community of Muslims) and national unity among Muslim and non-Muslim citizens of the modern nation state."[34] Christians genuinely feel that their religious and sociopolitical rights would be severely restricted under a Shari'a system of governance. Apart from this, just as Muslims are resentful of what they regard as the imposition of non-Islamic values on them, so too do Christians feel about any enforcement of the Shari'a within a shared geographical space. In this case both Christians and Muslims need to move the discussion beyond the Western, Christian democracy versus Arab-Islamic shariacracy. It is futile for African Christians and Muslims to lock themselves into a shariacracy versus democracy debate. In fact, the debate as it is conducted now is between caricatures of both Shari'a and secular democracy. For Christians, the Shari'a is about amputating limbs and flogging; for Muslims, secularism is about irreligious, immoral, and even antireligious values.[35] But as Archbishop Desmond Tutu has insisted, a secular state does not mean one that is without religion: "A secular state is not a godless or immoral one. It is one in which the state does not owe allegiance to any particular religion and thus no religion has an unfair advantage, or has privileges denied to others."[36]

This mutual misinformation apart, it seems that, while both Christians and Muslims are passionate about what they do not want, there is little or no evidence that they know what they really want. Christians do not seem to have any alternative of their own and so tend to seek refuge in a secular democracy that most know very little about. For their part, the Muslims who took to the streets in 2000 chanting for the introduction of the Shari'a in its entirety in northern Nigeria had little knowledge of what they were demanding. There was, for instance, very little or no internal discussion on what form of Shari'a best suits the twenty-first-century West African context. In fact, prior to the introduction of the Shari'a in northern Nigerian states, there was hardly any intra-Muslim discussion on which school of law (madhhab) should be followed, let alone whether the Shari'a as contained in the classical formulations should be "restored" or reworked, taking into account the unique West African collective experience. One would have thought that this is a fundamental question that Muslims should have resolved before embarking on the drive to enforce the Shari'a. For, as a proverb in my local Kusaal language has it, "it is only sensible to remove the thorn in the buttocks in order to sit properly and remove the one under the foot." But, as the English adage has it, better late than never! Muslims seem to now be engaged in that discussion. Ibrahim Sulaiman, who in earlier writings talked about "the eternal, unalterable model," now realizes that

> the key to success lies in how ultimately the Shari'a itself is nurtured and applied. What is being done so far is a mere restoration of the corpus of laws and regulations developed several centuries ago. Law, to be effective and relevant, must be a continuous evolution. Therefore, mere restoration of Shari'a is not enough, and will never serve any purpose. A process of construction of any system of law similar to the one undertaken by the founders of the early schools of law is the least that can be expected of the Umma. Any attempt to evade this responsibility by hiding behind the schools of law will fail. This is a different age, a different society and a different world. A different legal process responsive to the peculiarities and unique characteristics of this age, this society and this strange world is an absolute and inescapable necessity. The founders of the schools were merely performing their duties to their society. They never intended to solve the problems of generations yet to come, of which they knew nothing, neither did they ever claim that the results of their output were valid for all time. We have to do our duty to our society and our time. While we build on their legacy there must be a recognition that the eventual outcome of our work may almost amount to a new invention, not a replica.
>
> Finally, there must be a recognition of the fact that the Shari'a is first and foremost an idea, even before it is law. The Shari'a is a scholarly and intellectual process, liable to continuous growth and evolution. The scholarly and intellectual dimension of the Shari'a requires a much greater effort than the drive for its implementation.[37]

These internal discussions on both sides are very crucial in the search for the appropriate form of governance in West Africa. Both Christians and Muslims should first become properly informed about what they are commending to the other and, second, get informed about what the other is offering. Finally, we need to reexamine the premise on which the current debate is being conducted.

As far as some of us are concerned, the debate should not be about Shari'a and secular democracy. The issue that both Muslims and Christians need to explore together is to what extent we want to rely on the state to enforce matters of faith. We need to find out why and how, as deeply religious as Africans are, the office of the chief and that of the priest are kept separate in traditional societies. In probing these questions, Muslims and Christians have to bear in mind ibn Khaldun's advice that believers should be cautious in buying into the simplistic notion that religion and politics belong together, lest we "patch our worldly affairs by tearing our religion to pieces. Thus neither our religion lasts nor the worldly affairs we have been patching."[38] In the same vein, Lamin Sanneh cautions that "if religion looks to political power for its ultimate defence, then it will find in that its sole vindication and reward, and, in time, its demise."[39] These are wise words that we cannot afford to ignore.

Notes

1. This essay is reconstructed from an audio recording of the lecture given by Professor Ramadan at the Building Bridges seminar in Sarajevo.
2. Some would add to this a sixth: "dignity."
3. *Āl 'Imrān* (3) refers to aspects of the battle of Uḥud (625), in which the Muslims were defeated by the Meccan forces.
4. St. Thomas, *Summa Contra Gentiles* III, 146; cf. also *Summa Theologiae* 2a 2ae 64, 2.
5. St. Augustine, *De Civitate Dei* XV, 1.
6. Words attributed to the papal legate Arnaud at the sack of the city of Beziers during the Albigensian Crusade in 1209.
7. Chinua Achebe, *Things Fall Apart* (New York: Anchor, 1995), chap. 22 (1st ed., 1958).
8. Speech during the acceptance of the American Center for Democracy award, New York (United Nations, March 27, 1997—*Sjecanja: Autobiografski zapis*, Sarajevo: TKD Sahinpasic, 2001, 455).
9. *Islamski fundamentalizam: sta je to?* Sarajevo: Mesihat IZ u BiH, 1990, 209–10.
10. Magazine SAFF (Sarajevo), No. 138, February 15, 2005.
11. See www.malaysianinterfaithnetwork.net.
12. Part 1 of the 1957 constitution (Articles 1–4) is titled "The States, Religion and Law of the Federation," and Part 2 (Articles 5–13) "Fundamental Liberties."
13. 1957 constitution, Article 153.
14. Delivered at the Oxford Centre for Islamic Studies, April 16, 1996. The text is archived, with other speeches by Dr. Mahathir, on the official website of the prime minister of Malaysia: www.pmo.gov.my.
15. 1957 constitution, Article 160.
16. Ali Mazrui, "Shariacracy and Federal Models in the Era of Globalization: Nigeria in Comparative Perspective," International Conference on Shariah, organized by Nigerian Muslim Forum UK, London, April 14, 2001, www.shariah2001.nmnonline.net/ibrahim_paper.htm (accessed January 15, 2007).
17. Ali Mazrui, *The Africans: A Triple Heritage* (London: BBC, 1986), 19ff.
18. Ibraheem Sulaiman, "Sharia Restoration in Nigeria: The dynamics and the Process," International Conference on Shariah, www.shariah2001.nmnonline.net/ibrahim_paper.htm.

19. Ibraheem Sulaiman, "Islam and Secularism in Nigeria: An Encounter of Two Civilizations," *Impact International* (October 10–23, 1986): 8.

20. Ali Mazrui, "African Islam and Comprehensive Religion: Between Revivalism and Expansion," in *Islam in Africa: Proceedings of the Islam in Africa Conference,* ed. Nura Alkali, Adamu Adamu, Awwal Yadudu, Rashid Moten, and Haruna Salihi (Ibadan: Spectrum, 1993), 259.

21. Ali Mazrui, "Shariacracy and Federal Models."

22. Ismail al-Faruqi, comments in *Christian Mission and Islamic Da'wah: Proceedings of the Chambésy Dialogue Consultation* (Leicester: Islamic Foundation, 1982), 87.

23. Ibraheem Sulaiman, "Islam and Secularism in Nigeria," 9.

24. In N. Alkali et al., eds., *Islam in Africa,* 432–33.

25. J. Hunwick, "Sub-Saharan Africa and the Wider World of Islam: Historical and Contemporary Perspectives," in *African Islam and Islam in Africa: Encounters between Sufis and Islamists,* ed. D. Westerlund and E. E. Rosander (London: Hurst, 1997), 41 (emphasis added).

26. See www.shariah2001.nmnonline.net/ibrahim_paper.htm (accessed January 15, 2007).

27. Auwalu Hamisu Yadudu, "Benefits of Shariah and Challenges of Reclaiming a Heritage," International Shariah Conference, www.shariah 2001.nmnonline.net/ibrahim_paper.htm (accessed January 15, 2007).

28. Lamido Sanusi, "The Sharia: A Moslem Intervention," www.nmnon line.net (accessed January 15, 2007).

29. Lamin Sanneh, *Piety and Power: Muslims and Christians in West Africa* (New York: Orbis Books, 1996), 129.

30. Rabiatu Ammah, "Building God's Peace and Justice Together," in *The Road Ahead: A Christian-Muslim Dialogue,* ed. Michael Ipgrave (London: Church House, 2002), 98.

31. Bert Breiner, "A Christian View of Human Rights in Islam," CSIC Papers, no. 5 (April 1992): 4.

32. Alkali et al., eds., *Islam in Africa,* 432.

33. Breiner, "Christian View of Human Rights in Islam," pp. 7ff.

34. Abdullahi Ahmed an-Na'im, "Islam and Human Rights in Sahelian Africa," in *African Islam and Islam in Africa,* ed. Westerlund and Rosander, 89.

35. See, for instance, Sanusi, "Sharia."

36. Archbishop Desmond Tutu, comments in *Constitutional Talk,* official newsletter of the [South African] Constitutional Assembly, supplement to *Cape Times,* July 12, 1995.

37. Sulaiman, "Shari'a Restoration in Nigeria." Even leading Islamist schol-
    ars such as Sayyid Qutb of the Muslim Brotherhood of Egypt and Hasan
    al-Turabi of Sudan have expressed similar views with regard to the
    Shari'a.

38. See Franz Rosenthal, *Al-Muqaddimah: An Introduction to History,* vol. 1
    (Princeton, NJ: Princeton University Press, 1967), 427.

39. Sanneh, *Piety.*

Chapter 3

‹›

Caring Together for the World We Share

The four essays presented in this chapter all address, in light of the Christian and Muslim faiths, the interaction of human communities with the world all share. While rooted in the distinctive affirmations of their respective religious traditions, all four can be described as being in the broad sense ecumenical in that their field of vision is the whole inhabited world, the *oikoumene*. Moreover, they focus on two particularly urgent areas of concern that arise from humans' dwelling together in the shared home, the *oikos*, which is the world. Thus Rowan Williams and Tim Winter both tackle the theological challenge of poverty that is at the heart of *oiko-nomia*, the economics according to which the resources of the common home are allocated and managed. Ellen Davis and Aref Nayed both point to the need for a scripturally informed *oiko-logia*, an ecological understanding that will resource humanity in facing the developing environmental crisis.

Rowan Williams begins by setting out a wide definition of poverty; in light of the pattern of flourishing human community as revealed in the mission of Jesus and the life of the church, poverty is understood as the deprivation of individuals and groups of people from the participation and meaning that God wills for his world. In terms of economic strategies, Williams points to the pedagogical role of religious communities in holding this vision before the world. This is paradoxically exemplified in the vocation of some Christians (and Muslims) to voluntary poverty as a way of challenging the assumption that human value consists solely in material security, but it can also be seen in ventures such as microcredit initiatives, in sustained reflection on the ethical principles of investment and development, and in keeping alive in wider public discourse a holistic account of human well-being. In all these areas, Christians and Muslims have been entrusted with a common agenda to explore and pursue together.

Tim Winter recalls the option for the poor displayed by the saints of the Islamic tradition, sometimes in opposition to the established political order of their times. Their option for the poor was in turn rooted in a personal option for poverty informed by the example of the apostolic life of the Prophet himself. Winter goes on to trace a radical, and always contested, tradition of reflection in Judaism, Christianity, and Islam that looks to Abraham and his heirs—Winter shows how in Islam the transmission of this tradition is focused particularly through the figure of Ishmael—to find embodied there a principle of sharing and solidarity that is expressed through poverty and that is strongly oriented toward the continuing quest for justice. In the current inequality and turbulence of the world, he argues, Christians and Muslims can, and must, reclaim from their tradition a radical option for the poor.

Ellen Davis powerfully recovers from the Hebrew Scriptures the sharp and terrifying vision of a world being reduced through human irresponsibility to a state of formless waste. The effect of genuine prophetic speech, she points out, is to challenge the apathetic inability to be astonished by this crisis; for the human community to be restored to its proper place, the tragic imagination must first be reawakened so that humans can learn again a sense of their radical vulnerability. Positively, Davis demonstrates that underpinning creation, and increasingly violated by our actions, is a covenanted order within which divine instruction assigns humans a prescribed place. Good faith in the face of the environmental crisis is to be found in recognizing this divine givenness of the world and in seeking to live within it as creatures guided by the Creator.

Aref Nayed argues that a responsible Islamic approach to environmental issues must be built from two key Qur'anic concepts: *āya*, "sign," and *raḥma*, "compassion." To see the world "āyatologically" is to interpret it as an interlocking set of signs that open out toward one another and toward the ultimate reality of God. To set this semiotic matrix in the context of "raḥmatology" is to trace the motivation of all creation back to its source in the divine compassion. *Āya* and *raḥma* in turn require a right response from humans as their interpreters and recipients: rather than seeing the world as just a collection of "things" to be manipulated to our advantage, they are to stand before them with thanksgiving and appreciation for the *raḥma* of the God who addresses them through his *āyāt* in creation.

While they evidently differ considerably in method and in scope, these four presentations have two features in common in their underlying structure. First, they all ground their approach to current economic and ecological questions in a theological starting point, a vision of the world as charged by God with a meaning that is received by humans as a gift. Second, they convey the sharpness of the prophetic challenge that responding rightly to that gift requires of us, particularly in our divided and threatened world. It is precisely because their motivations are so deeply rooted in their different spiritual visions of the world that Christians and Muslims need to act together in practical ways to call human society back to God's purpose for its common home.

Christianity, Islam, and the Challenge of Poverty

ℰℐ

Rowan Williams

I t is likely that religious believers of all traditions would begin by warning
that *poverty* is not a word with a single definition. We may think first of
apparently straightforward material deprivation—a low income, no public welfare or emergency provision, poor health care, and inability to afford basics
such as food. But behind this lies a set of more deep-rooted concerns about the
lack of access to power—power, that is, which can be used to change one's
situation. It is a commonplace now that the problem of poverty is inseparable
from the ways in which a global economy can dictate the terms on which a
nation's economy behaves: It is bound up with debt, with protectionist practices that make it impossible for a nation to enter the international markets on
fair terms, with the way that the presence of multinational companies can affect
the free operation of local elected governments. And deeper still there is the
level at which poverty has to be thought about in terms of resources not easy
to quantify—the stability of a domestic or an educational environment, access
to unpolluted natural space, and familiarity with the practices and languages
that offer access to human meaning.

Poverty is the widowed woman struggling to feed an orphaned grandchild
in Malawi or South Africa. It is the child abducted from home to fight in an
insurgent army in Uganda or Myanmar. It is the politician in Central America
or Eastern Europe trying to balance budgets for hospitals or schools in a falter-
ing and debt-laden economy. It is the citizen paralyzed by a culture of endemic
corruption, disabled by pollution, trapped in working practices that undermine
family and a stable community—and this last is not restricted to the poorer
countries of the world. So it is also the modern Western person cut off from

the depths of religious and cultural meaning by a series of relentless messages about consumer gratification.

Our religious traditions thus have a double responsibility in such a context. They define what human community looks like when it is properly in accord with God's character and purpose, and they challenge what it is that holds back human communities from living in such a way. In the Christian perspective, the definition of human community is worked out primarily in the context of the historical mission of Jesus and subsequently through St. Paul's theology of the body of Christ, and in what follows I want to trace the development of this definition to see how it confronts the particular crises of our own day in regard to poverty. It is important to do this sort of work if we are to avoid an approach to poverty that is essentially just about benevolence to those who suffer material deprivation. Basic as this may seem to be, the truth is that Christianity, like other faiths, has a more nuanced and more positive contribution to make, with a distinctive doctrinal content. In the context of inter faith encounter, we need to bring to the surface how our actual beliefs shape what we do—not simply to agree that kindness is better than cruelty.

As the Gospels present it to us, the mission of Jesus of Nazareth is about the way in which the community of God's people—historically, the Jewish people who had first received the law and the covenant—is being re-created in relation to Jesus himself. He is consistently concerned with those who have no voice or standing among the people—not only the materially poor but also those who have no chance of satisfying the full demands of the ceremonial law and those who are despised because of sickness or sin. When someone responds to Jesus in trust, when someone receives healing from him, the effect is that they are, according to Jesus, set free to take their full place among God's chosen, free to worship and offer sacrifice and to be confident that they have an indestructible value in God's eyes. Because of that sense of their value, they will be free from anxiety about material things and free to take certain risks in order to make known to others the promise that Jesus offers. Thus they are able to live in a community that is not constantly threatened and divided by rivalry and acquisitiveness; they are able to offer each other a love that is like the love given by Jesus in God's name.

In such a community, it is unthinkable that any particular person should be left as a victim without voice or power, with their destiny decided by others. The community itself may be a community that adopts a level of material poverty as a matter of calling, but this is clearly different from a situation where such privation is imposed because of the greed of others. And the commitment to refrain from passing judgment on others or insulting them means that no one is deprived of respect. This is a community that counteracts poverty in the sense that it resists whatever it is that denies a voice to people and draws all together in a shared possibility of offering acceptable worship to God.

For Christians the crucial fact is that the community established by Jesus in his ministry is restored after his crucifixion, when he is raised to life. And more than that: His death, seen as the perfect offering of sacrificial, worshipping obedience to God, establishes the possibility of a community that shares in Jesus's own intimacy with God, breaking down the barrier between earth and heaven. Hence the whole community becomes a sort of extension of God's presence in Jesus—the body of Christ—and, because all have the dignity belonging to those God regards as his children, it is a natural development that St. Paul speaks of the body of Christ as the place where all are given gifts by the spirit of God to share with the entire community. To each and every Christian believer is given the dignity of being a "giver"; the believer does not receive gifts for his or her own sake or use but receives an active capacity to shape the character of the community by what is bestowed on him or her by God.

St. Paul, in his second letter to Corinth, spells this out further in the eighth and ninth chapters, where he urges some of the Christian communities to be generous to others so that they may also have the chance to be generous in return. The nature of Christian giving here is seen as the sowing of seed—that is, the beginning of a process of growth. It is not simply the alleviation of a problem; it creates something, the possibility of reciprocal action. The community in tune with God's will is one in which all have a role that is in some sense creative, positive. It is therefore a community in which many of the various kinds of poverty identified earlier should not be visible. Whatever the level of material prosperity, what will be typical of the Christian group is that it seeks ways of making all members participants in the common work of shaping its life so that it can be a visible image of God's purpose for humanity. It is definitely not a matter of (to use the dismissive phrase often heard) "throwing money" at the poor; it is treating the less advantaged as potentially your own associates and helpers (and perhaps rescuers). And it also takes for granted the basic belief that pervades Paul's letters—that the privation or suffering of any one part of the body is the privation of all. To help the poor to a capacity for action and liberty is something essential for one's own health as well as theirs: there is a needful gift they have to offer that cannot be offered so long as they are confined by poverty.

Christianity and Islam alike have a long tradition of commending alms-giving, the practice of simple instinctive generosity to the poor. But while this is a given in the tradition, it should not be assumed for Christianity any more than for Islam that this is all that can be said about a proper response of faith when confronted by poverty. The Jewish vision, so clearly set out in the "Jubi-lee" vision of Leviticus, is one that refuses to accept an infinite spiral of acquisi-tion on the one hand and deprivation on the other;[1] it assumes instead that God's people will have institutions that seek to control this spiral and to check from time to time that some members of the community are not suffering long-term exclusion from the freedoms of ordinary economic stability. Both Christianity and Islam inherit something of this vision.

It is the same vision that equips them to resist the poverty that can charac-terize cultural life and personal relations. In emphasizing the significance of faithful marriage partnership, for example, they resist that corrosive form of poverty that deprives children of security. In taking tradition seriously, they provide a hinterland of human resource, a sense of the proper relativity of the present moment and the need to explore indebtedness to the depth of history. We might try to sum up this part of the argument simply by observing that our traditions do not in fact treat poverty as a matter of material security that can be remedied by a transfer of material resources; they begin with a picture of human capacity under God and human community as it is formed by the act or call of God and on the basis of this find themselves combating many differ-ent varieties of poverty in the name of a vision of free interdependence. Our care for our common social space today needs to have this notion at its heart.

How does this appear in light of the various problems posed by the global-ized economy? And what actual strategies do or should we adopt in making faith's resistance to poverty effective?

For the Christian, there is a central paradox in some of the language of the gospels and the Christian tradition. Accepting voluntary poverty is a thoroughly positive thing in this language. But it is seen as a specific manifestation of that letting go of anxiety about material security that is the outward mark of a life lived in comprehensive trust in God's acceptance. The person who accepts the calling to poverty—in monastic life, to take the obvious example—does not thereby say that material deprivation is good but that material prosperity and comfort is something whose absence can embody a lesson about inner freedom, when it is freely surrendered. The voluntarily poor person does not declare that involuntary poverty has to be endured; the lesson is rather to the wealthy. Human life and value do not depend on the unlimited ability to accumulate material security.

This vocation is therefore part of that pedagogy by which the prosperous are challenged—as in II Corinthians—to give, not in a way that makes them paupers but in a way that equips the poor to begin to have a reciprocal relation with them. The surrender of some part of their freedom on the part of the prosperous works toward a real mutuality, not just a reversal of the roles of rich and poor. It is thus true that "wealth creation" can be described as a proper Christian aim if it is clearly directed toward the creation of increasing numbers of persons who have the freedom to join in the process. And this, incidentally, ought to be the light in which we approach the vexed question of "free trade" and "fair trade." The proper equipping of a poor nation to take a substantial part in the global economy through an open market is in principle entirely good. It is perfectly true that trade is a tool of prosperity. However, the forcing of the pace of trade liberalization produces social cost that may threaten the longer-term welfare of a nation, and it is a standing outrage that "free trade" is commended to economically vulnerable nations by other nations who persist in protectionism. It has to be said clearly and often that the religious objection to aspects of the current global trade regime is not a sentimental aversion to wealth or a sort of commendation of endless large-scale almsgiving. Rather, it has to do with the ways in which certain practices make it impossible for some nations to be economic agents in a meaningful way.

It is likely, then, that religious believers will be found among those who are skeptical of appeals to the market as the primary agent of benevolent change; but they will also be found among those who seek to encourage the kind of enterprise that creates wealth in the form of employment, which represents increased levels of control and capacity in a social environment. Perhaps one of the most distinctive contributions that can be made by religious communities is the active encouragement of local credit schemes. Whether in the shape of the Anglican "Five Talents" initiative in Africa or the Grameen banks of Muhammad Yunus in South Asia, there is a way of furthering economic maturity that belongs most obviously with religious conviction simply because it assumes that a dependable local community, bound by trust and common commitment, is an ideal unit in which economic empowerment can take place.

Not much is gained simply by religious groups' and religious leaders' repeating slogans about the costs and evils of globalization. But if they can learn to work together in encouraging microcredit initiatives that make persons and small communities into real economic agents, they will be doing something profoundly worthwhile. They will be assisting people to exercise the creative responsibility that is God's gift and purpose for human beings.

Similarly, on the international stage, we need more open and sophisticated consultation between Christian and Muslim teachers and leaders on the ethical principles of investment and development. When we get beyond the standoff between "free trade" and "fair trade" we will have made real progress, and this can only happen if we have a robust sense of what economic activity is meant to deliver in the long run—which is not wealth in the usual narrow sense of material abundance for certain persons but the liberty to make and sustain a stable, dependable environment for human growth.

Economists are beginning to acknowledge that measures of national wealth and poverty in terms strictly of average income tell you little that is significant to the health or viability of a society. Wealth itself has to be redefined (as hinted earlier) to mean access to the resources that make our existence stable and meaningful—so that material abundance created at the expense of such access and at the expense of cultural or family stability or the presence of the signs of faith in public life will represent a net move toward poverty. And—to indicate issues that will be dealt with in another essay—the loss of access to an unpolluted physical environment is likewise a net decrease in wealth, as argued by economists such as Partha Dasgupta.

It is impossible to deny that Christians and Muslims have a common agenda here: both faiths have at their heart the living image of a community raised up by God's call to reveal to the world what God's purpose is for humanity. That is, both turn away from any simply individual idea of the good life. Both are thus inevitably drawn to reflection on how the life of society can be molded to the life that God desires for human flourishing. Historically and theologically, they have offered very different solutions, with Christianity keeping a more obvious gap between the visible community of the church and the institutions of the state, and Islam normally working on the assumption that the good society is one in which divine law is directly realized. Both, however, have a necessarily critical stance toward a society that has no means of limiting rivalry and acquisition or that tolerates indefinitely habits and practices that deny to large numbers the possibility of exercising that freedom to be creative in social matters that we have seen to be so important in religious speech.

They will therefore be on the lookout for opportunities for a particular sort of collaboration—not primarily in the defense of religion in a secular context, though there may well be circumstances where that is desirable, but in the defense of a certain vision of what properly belongs to human agents. They will be advocates locally of institutions that build trust and capacity and internationally of institutions that safeguard a level playing field in economic exchange and limit unaccountable economic power. They will also be advocates for the "visibility" of religion. In the pluralist societies of modern Europe, this cannot mean religious dominance; the near panic that afflicts some secularists at the notion of the visible and audible participation of religious groups in public discourse reflects an unhappy historical memory of times when the church assumed an ideological monopoly. But things have changed. It is not that we have to resist extravagant claims for public religious authority; the problem now is more that we have to resist the potentially tyrannical assumption that the secular perspective is so obviously normative that religious commitment should not be publicly visible. And to resist this is certainly not to defend the rights of institutions; it is to defend, rather, the right of a society to have access to meaning. It is an inseparable part of the struggle of faith against poverty of every kind. Believers will affirm that public ignorance of the language of faith is a civic deprivation: It denies people the most radical perspective possible on their present existence and robs them of the most persistent and indestructible ground for constructive criticism of any status quo.

One final observation may be in order. A situation where religious and ethnic rivalries obscure this common commitment to address poverty, material and spiritual, represents a luxury in the world that is emerging. Our faith commitments are, of course, different, and our truth claims are not simply compatible. But we do share a world, one that is scarred by all the varieties of poverty I have sketched and more, and one that is threatened by environmental disaster of an unprecedented kind. We shall continue to debate our truth claims; a global ethic for today is not one in which we dissolve our differences in a liberal consensus. But we all begin from the belief that human welfare is not something that can be sorted out by pragmatism and human goodwill alone; we begin from the beliefs of a called community, charged with showing God to God's creation. Our patterns of holiness are often different, though they also converge in unexpected and challenging ways; yet our sense of what makes for health in common life is, just as often, close enough for conversation and for common work. If the "secular" is always at risk of forgetting the nonnegotiable value of the other (the other person, the material world) in the eyes of the Creator, we have a calling we can all make sense of. We know where the roots of poverty lie—in the refusal to accept the meaning that God gives the world, a refusal that shows itself not only in atheism but also in the anxious and greedy spirit that cannot see the human context of economic activity. Against this, we appeal to the law of God made plain to us—for Christians, made flesh for us in the Savior, implanted in the body of Christ, which is the church. What our faiths have to offer, not least in divided and disadvantaged societies, is quite simply a different depth of resource for human hope.

Poverty and the Charism of Ishmael

Timothy J. Winter

B osnian folklore, that treasury of cross-grained wisdom, seems to favor two themes above all others: saints and plum brandy. The very best kind of story is often one that combines the two. An example is the tale of the seventeenth century Qadiri dervish, Ḥasan Kaimije. Kaimije was a figure known for his austerity, his name (the "Erect") recalling a forty-day retreat that he spent entirely in a standing position, and he gave his city a complex book of dry numerological speculations as well as a collection of Sufi poems. According to the story, he was once leaving his mosque on a windy night when his candle was extinguished by a sudden gust of wind, leaving him in utter darkness. He pointed his candle at the minaret, at which the candle miraculously began to burn again. "Oh, what have I done?" he cried. "I have discovered that I am a saint!" Fearful of sinful pride, he spent the rest of the night in a tavern. The next day, the outraged townsfolk drove him out of Sarajevo, and he was obliged to settle in Zvornik, where his tomb was to become an important way station on the old pilgrim road to Gül Baba, the Muslim saint of Budapest.

Whether Ḥasan Kaimije actually imbibed that night is a question that continues to divide his admirers from his detractors. Yet the issue seems to have been resolved, in a disappointing way, by modern historians. A more likely explanation for the dervish's banishment from the city, it emerges, was his involvement in the peasants' revolt of 1682. Outraged at the hoarding of grain by the city's burghers, villagers had rampaged through the streets, burning down the Muslim law court and murdering the chief judge and his assistant, whose interpretation of Islam seemed to have done nothing to reduce the miseries of a starving countryside.[2]

The poor, of course, are always with us. Men of religion, however, are not always with the poor. This is an unhappy reality in Muslim history, where *ulema* did not unfailingly fulfill their vocation as mediators of the people's grievances to a distant and unsympathetic sultan. Yet those of a Sufi persuasion could often play this role, and Kaimije is in numerous and distinguished company. Another such saint was his contemporary Sidi Lahsen Lyussy, a prophetic opponent of the Moroccan sultan's cruelty to laborers engaged in building a fortress. Invited to the palace, Lyussy deliberately broke the king's dinner service, plate by plate. The following conversation ensued:

> *"Salām 'alaykum."*
> *"Wa-'alaykum as-salām."*
> *"Sidi, we have been treating you like a guest of God, and you have broken all our dishes."*
> "Well, which is better—the pottery of God, or the pottery of clay?"

The sultan, refusing to improve the working conditions of his laborers, had the saint exiled from the city.[3]

Stories such as these were the standard fare of Muslim hagiography and played an important countercultural role in a static monarchical world where the official *ulema* were closely embedded in the hierarchy of society and were not always seen by the poor as natural allies. Today, in some Muslim countries, senior scholars continue to be appointed by the state and can appear more as instruments of official control of the population than as the people's representatives before the throne. Radicals of all stripes have been alienated accordingly, with sometimes violent results.

Among establishment and turbulent clerics alike, however, the point of reference remains the Prophet. And here, at the religion's heart, we find a consistent and challenging example of a man who not only denounced the miseries of poverty and took political sides with the poor but also joined them in his own manner of life. We might say that, for him, there could be no preferential option for the poor without a preferential option for poverty.

The Prophet's virtue is what Islam calls *zuhd*, which is usually rendered into English as "asceticism." We can cautiously accept this version, with two important provisos. First, that Islam cannot connect celibacy with renunciation, for, as al-Nawawi says, "all the desires harden the heart, with the exception of sexual desire, which softens it."[4] Second, his was not an asceticism of method, a *via purgativa*, as his proximity to God was already accomplished or rather had been given as part of the prophetic charism. His renunciation was not of things his physical self craved but appeared as the natural form of life of someone entranced by God. As Jalāl al-Dīn Rūmī puts it,

That poverty is not for the sake of avoiding entanglements.
No, it is there because nothing exists but God.[5]

In a representative piece of devotional writing, the modern scholar of Mecca, Shaykh Muḥammad ʿAlawī al-Mālikī, describes him as the perfect *zāhid*, the flawless exemplar of holy poverty. Mālikī's treatment takes its cue from a celebrated hadith found in the classical collections of Bukhārī and Muslim, which describes how the Prophet once rose from a rush mat on which he had been sleeping, with marks visible on his shoulder. The companions asked whether in future they could spread something less hard for him to sleep on, but he replied, "What have I to do with this world? Towards this world, my likeness is that of a wayfarer travelling on a summer day, who rests in the afternoon beneath a tree, and then moves on, leaving it behind."[6]

The scriptural proof texts listed by Mālikī tell how months would pass without a cooking fire being lit in his house. He ate only barley bread, never bread from wheat flour. He had only one set of clothes and sandals. When engaged in hard physical labor he would tie a flat stone to his stomach to reduce the pangs of hunger. He would never eat more than one kind of food at a private meal in his house: If it were dates, he would not touch bread. God offered to turn the mountains of Mecca into gold for him, but he prayed: "No, O Lord; but I shall hunger for a day, and be satisfied the next; so that when I am satisfied, I shall praise and thank You, and when I hunger, I shall humble myself to You and pray."[7]

The best known of all Prophetic panegyric poems, the "Mantle-Ode" (*al-Burda*) of al-Būṣīrī (d. c. 1294), shows how central this principle of holy poverty became to his medieval image. The rhetorical progression of the poem begins with an evocation of nostalgia for the lost homeland, followed by an explanation of how that homeland has been lost through the pursuit of vain passion, and then proposes the Prophet as the sure guide. In our perplexity and world intoxication, only a renunciation as radical as his will awaken us to the miraculous nature of prophecy and sainthood, which alone can put an end to our exile. So Būṣīrī writes, re-creating his own moment of repentance:

Ẓalamtu sunnata man aḥyaʾẓ-ẓalāma ilā
an ishtakat qadamāhuʾḍ-ḍurra min warami.[8]

I have wronged the way of he who brought life to the dark night,
to the point that his feet would swell painfully [due to his night vigils].

Wa-shadda min saghabin aḥshāʾahu wa-ṭawā,
Taḥtaʾl-ḥijārati kashḥan mutrafaʾl-adami.[9]

He tied [a length of cloth] over his stomach, from hunger,
His waist emaciated, beneath a stone.

This image of the Prophet's apostolic poverty was recurrent and irreproachably sourced, yet it gave rise to several arguments.[10] The first concerned the reason for his anger over the poverty of others. The Qurʾan urges the feeding of the poor and denounces those who are indifferent to their misery (*al-Balad* 90:14; *al-Insān* 76:8; *Quraysh* 106:4; etc). It decrees the feeding of ten paupers as the expiation for a violated oath (*al-Māʾida* 5:89). A share of the sacrificial meat at the *ḥajj* pilgrimage is to be given to the poor (*al-Ḥajj* 22:36), while *zakāt* monies are primarily to be used for the relief of poverty (*al-Tawba* 9:60). Hence the religion's basic structures and commandments massively internalize charitable giving for the alleviation of hunger and poverty, which are seen as primary social evils. Yet the Prophet himself was poor and, moreover, had chosen poverty, as his position of political authority in Medina offered him access, had he so wished, to considerable treasure. His was, as Mālikī repeats, *faqr ikhtiyār*, not *faqr iḍṭirār*, voluntary, not involuntary, poverty; so that the next line in Būṣīrī's poem runs:

Wa-rāwadathuʾl-jibāluʾsh-shummu min dhahabin
ʿan nafsihi fa-arāhā ayyamā shamami.[11]

The lofty mountains, become gold, sought to tempt him,
away from his soul; but he showed them such disdain.

This was in lived solidarity with the poor of Medina: He would not sleep at night until any food and coins that might remain in his house had been given to the poor.[12] It was also, as Rūmī sees it, because the true lover may become detached from all save the beloved; even though, in his case, he was in the very middle of the world by virtue of his prophetic office.[13] This is *khalwat dar anjumān*, solitude in the multitude, which includes a personal detachment from a deprivation whose presence in others may arouse the prophetic wrath.

If the Prophet opposed poverty in his world, yet cultivated it in his own life, in what sense is it part of a Muslim *imitatio*? Should it be classed with the genre of Prophetic practices known as *khaṣā'iṣ*, duties applicable to him alone, from which his community is exempt? The *tahajjud* prayer, for instance, was an obligation for him, and he spent hours in prayer every night. For his followers, it was merely a recommended practice: *sunna* not *fard*. The *wiṣāl* fast, in which he refrained from eating at sundown but continued fasting through the night, was permissible to him but unlawful to his community. This genre has always intrigued the commentators, given the religion's general emphasis on Prophetic emulation, and some lengthy discussions have ensued.[14]

Whether or not they took the intensity of the Prophet's renunciation to be a binding precedent, most medieval Muslim scholars were sure about the general preferability of poverty over wealth. Al-Ghazālī, in his treatment of the subject, takes this to be the clear sense of the Prophet's statement that "the poor of my community shall enter paradise five hundred years before the rich,"[15] and of another hadith which runs: "shall I not tell you who shall be the kings of Paradise? Every weak, oppressed one, marked by dust and unkempt hair, noticed by no-one."[16] Yet Ghazālī also warns us against the dangers of a false adherence to poverty, a lethal danger in some Sufi circles, where the patched robe had become a temptation to vainglory. The sincere wealthy are better than the greedy poor. *Zuhd*, he concludes, is to renounce the world from conviction as to its insignificance when compared to the preciousness of the next; as for a Muslim who renounces its temptations for any other reason, he is no kind of *zāhid*.[17] And extremism in this, as in all else, is unacceptable to God.[18]

This Ghazālīan perspective turns out to be the mainstream one in Islamic piety. The word *faqr*, "poverty," is linked to an ancient Arabian word for "back," because poverty is the breaking of one's back. If this condition is chosen, as part of a process of spiritual purgation or from simple love of God, it lies at the heart of religion; if forced on others who cannot bear it, it is a deadly crime. For the Prophet also says, "Were poverty to be a man, I would slay him," and prays to God to preserve him from "a poverty that causes forgetfulness, or a wealth that causes tyranny."[19] In other words, the poverty that breaks the back of the human spirit is of the devil, but the poverty that breaks the back of the ego is of God. The sign of the latter's presence is the love of God.

Here is Ḥasan Kaimije, in ecstatic mood, coupling the pain that lies in being weaned from worldliness with joy at the approach to God:

> O my heart, desire grief in this world today. Be ill, be poor, today!
> He who is not grief-stricken today, shall weep forever and fall into calamity.
> But he who leaves the world behind on a night journey, shall ascend with Aḥmad
>   today.[20]

For Kaimije, Aḥmad's shrine, the Ka'ba, is the site of the binding of Abraham's son. When God sees our utter renunciation and our acceptance of his decree, an unimaginable future begins.[21]

At this point, having indicated some of the tensions and debates within the Muslim tradition, I offer some thoughts on their application to our present world. And I attempt this by considering, or reconsidering, the figure of Abraham and the specifically Ishmaelite hue of the Ka'ba's religion.

Oddly, given the fact (an arguable fact, perhaps) that the Jesus of the Gospels is a less ascetic figure than the Muhammad of the hadiths, Islamic culture has loved to associate *zuhd* with Jesus;[22] this is certainly the case with Ḥasan Kaimije, who sees what he calls *tecrīdlik*, the radical stripping away of attachments, as a significantly Christic possibility:

> Having renounced, we embark on the journey,
> We have inclined towards Jesus today.[23]

Yet the endlessly fertile Genesis story of Abraham has had different repercussions for the way Muslims and Christians have seen and received the world, both as history and as creation of God. Abraham is anti-idolatrous in both cases. In both traditions, and for the rabbis also, he is a breaker of the idols in the soul, the attachments that prevent us from surrendering to God. Yet in Islam he possesses an additional Meccan dimension. It is, finally, not for Christian reasons that Kaimije, who sings of Jesus, joins the bread riot in Sarajevo.

In a well-known meditation on Abraham, Emmanuel Levinas contrasts the patriarch with Ulysses. Abraham has migrated from his homeland into an alterity that is thereby affirmed; Ulysses, the European and hence the Pauline Christian, leaves alterity and returns to his home. Unlike Abraham, home is his destiny. In Europe, there is resolution, the closing of a circuit that brings redemption. The New Israel becomes a bounded homeland, an eschatological space. Alterity lies outside this city and is fallen, while the homeland, which for Levinas signifies ontology, is regained and considered universal.[24] Here, Levinas thinks, is the core distinction between Jewish and Christian readings of the "knight of faith." As he writes: "It is in the impurity of the world, which the Old Testament takes on together with all its facts, that purity is made. But it is made, it is an act. There is no redemption of the world, only a transformation of the world. Self-redemption is already an action; purely inner repentance is a contradiction in terms. Suffering has no magical effect. The just man who suffers is worthy not because of his suffering, but because of his justice, which defies suffering."[25] It is not simply that the great self-renunciation, prefigured by Abraham, which launches Christianity has not, in practice, recognizably redeemed the world.[26] It is that redemption itself is un-Abrahamic, being implicitly predicated on a polarity of Self and Other. What is required is justice. As he adds, polemically: "It is in economic justice that man glimpses the face of man. Has Christianity itself found a horizon for its generosity other than in famine and drought?"[27]

Levinas's project, a post-Holocaust one, then casts Judaism as the opponent of any scheme to redeem the world, something that, he thinks, will be grounded in an inexorably dichotomizing logic. Instead, one is to strive for justice, and for economic justice in particular, while acknowledging the Hebrew Bible's sense of the nonperfectibility of the world.

Such a dichotomy between the intentions of the Christian and the Jewish Abrahams is certainly arguable, and it is hard to resist pointing out the irony of a philosophy that decries any resolution in one's apprehension of the other while offering so substantial a polemic against what it takes to be the essence of another faith. Perhaps his abrasiveness here is no more than part of his necessarily bitter reaction to Simone Weil. He has not adequately seen that attitudes diverge within Christianity, partly due to the ambiguity of the church's situation between Pentecost and Parousia. Is Christianity to be fully proleptic, a realized eschatology in which there is justice and plenty, validly; or is it to be a new Israel in the sense that it must renounce, and sacrifice, for the true society that only the Second Coming can inaugurate? But we should let that be and instead consider where Islam's Abraham might place us within this imagined polarity.

Safet Bektović has helpfully pointed out some of the differences between Islamic readings of Abraham and those shared or disputed between Jews and Christians.[28] But to his analysis we would add the comment that Islam's Abraham, that great archetype of renunciation of home and family, does not simply migrate into alterity, as Levinas proposes, but returns home; not to Chaldea, of course, but to the Great Sanctuary, the ancient place of worship established by Adam. Unlike Ulysses he revisits an unsuspected home, discovering that Ithaca was an illusion and his yearning for it a false or metaphorical nostalgia: Penelope is merely another Circe. His renunciation of homeland/Self does not compel an eternal irresolution. Hence he is not the Levinassian Abraham, champion of aporia and leader of "the merciless war declared by the Bible and the Talmud on the sacred and sacraments."[29] Nor is he the Christian Abraham, whose readiness to sacrifice his son inaugurates a people that is the prototype of the church, which is to be a true city of justice within an unredeemed world. This Abraham is "neither Christian nor Jew, but a primordial monotheist, a Muslim" (*al-Baqara* 2:135). The Great Sanctuary that he builds up and reconsecrates is a reminder of the primordial, cosmic covenant.[30] His is a migration back to the "place" where all souls affirmed God. The temper of Islam, therefore, acknowledges the world's nonperfectibility and awaits (though mildly) the Parousia, but by building itself on a reminder of humanity's original grace seeks to transform the world with an Ishmaelite law, a law for the poor, in which relief of the unfortunate, through the *zakāt* and other institutions, is legally enforced and is not left only to private charity.[31] As the Meccan scripture commands: "*Take* alms of their wealth, so that you may purify and sanctify them" (*al-Tawba* 9:103). The rejection of primogeniture and the prohibition of usury are nothing but accessories to this project of disaggregating wealth.

There is a second departure from the Genesis story. The Bible speaks of Ishmael but is concerned primarily with Isaac and his descendants. The scripture that appears in the Meccan sanctuary affirms Isaac's covenant but is to be an Ishmaelite manifesto. Ishmael, recorded in the Qur'ān as the builder of the Ka'ba, with his father (*al-Baqara* 2:127), is buried in the Meccan temple, beside his mother, the Gentile matriarch Hagar, and his daughters.[32] It is in this sanctuary, with its overwhelmingly Ishmaelite ambience, that the prophet of poverty receives his first revelations, which include some of the Qur'an's most searching indictments of Meccan indifference to the poor, the weak, and the orphaned.

What is it to belong to the nation of Ishmael, the *Banī Ismā'īl*? Most obviously, his name indicates the virtue of hearing God and being heard by him. Ishmael is, at least for the later Muslim tradition, the son for whom a ram is substituted. But he is the site of a further sacrifice, one that has been neglected but is perhaps still more intriguing and difficult. He is banished, with his tragic mother, due to the jealousy of Sarah, an act that was hardly less certain a sentence of death than the *akedah* itself. Again, Abraham is choosing poverty at God's command, by divesting himself of his only irreplaceable assets: his sons.

This second sacrifice is one of the fertile enigmas of the book of Genesis. Hagar and Ishmael are guiltless, yet they are punished by an exile. In this they resemble their father more than Isaac does. Yet the authors of the text are clear about the salvation history; as Westermann's commentary concludes: "The expulsion of Ishmael limits the people which calls Abraham its father to the single line, the descendants of Isaac."[33] The attempted sacrifice of Isaac, which is not prefigured in his father, opens a covenant; the attempted sacrifice of Ishmael, which does echo his father's own trial, creates the symbol of the dead end, the withered branch, the dry root. God is with the privileged, not the outcast and the bereft. St. Paul drives this home in Galatians, where he repeats: "cast out the slave and her son, for the slave shall not inherit with the son of the free woman" (Gal. 4:22–30). This is, of course, said against the Jews, as Augustine understands, but today it seems to have reverted to its original Ishmaelite subject:[34] much current American rhetoric about "freedom" as opposed to various forms of Islam may credibly be traced back to such Biblical antinomies. Ishmael is in bondage to his law; the American is free in the spirit. For the ideologues of an American apotheosis of history, Ishmael is at best a kind of medieval foreshadowing; the writings of Bernard Lewis and others may praise premodern Muslim philosophy and social pluralism but remain clear that their fullness needed to wait for America. Here, again, we might recall Augustine's presentation of Hagar as the figuring of Sarah, who alone is the figuring of the fulfillment, the free city.[35]

Such a triumphalist vision of Isaac and Sarah, archetypes of privilege, as the ultimate legitimators and source of Western power and wealth will not commend itself to Muslims. Perhaps the great dichotomy between Islam and the West that is now, in places, expressing itself in violence, whether directed from Afghan caves or the Pentagon, is nothing other than the working out of this divine comedy. If this is so, and I am old-fashioned enough to believe that the scriptures (and not only my own) still give as well as receive, then Islam may need to think more clearly about the meaning of Ishmael and attempt a new theology of its current global humiliation that is rooted in the Prophet's dictum, "Poverty is my pride."

The Ishmaelite, quasi-egalitarian principle of sharing and solidarity is for Muslims a major component of theo-political action. Islam is often reproached for this, as were some liberation theologians under the last pope, but it is non-negotiable: Caesar must be placed under restraint. For most of its history Islam placed the relief of poverty and sickness in the hands not of a clerical class but of the entire believing community, which was itself "priestly," and whose political leaders were accountable in Shari'a law for the distribution to the poor of *zakāt* and the various religiously mandated tithes (*'ushr, kharāj*) on land and natural resources.[36] The *waqf* system furnished the bulk of poor relief, together with orphanages and free education and health care for the physically and mentally ill.[37]

Under modern conditions, with Islamic countries largely governed by elites who have converted to the values of the Western establishment and whose populations have suffered grievously following the abolition of the *waqf* system and publicly administered *zakāt* tithes, there is a pressing need to reinvigorate an Ishmaelite politics of the oppressed, and this need has been recognized and pursued by many Islamic leaders. Yet there is a difficulty here: Islamic teachings concerning times of great sedition and distress, most particularly the Great Wrath which precedes the End, insist on political disengagement, poverty, and isolation. The Prophet diagnosed the end times in terms of "time passing more quickly, religious knowledge dying away, covetousness prevailing, and civil strife."[38] Explaining the "covetousness," *shuḥḥ*, al-Qurṭubī comments, "This will be acceptable, it will be studied, recommended and invited to."[39] The God-fearing commandment will be to "snap your bows, break your bowstrings, and strike at stones with your swords; if any of you lives to see that time, let him be like the better of Adam's two sons."[40] Renunciation, too, is counseled: "The time has almost come when a Muslim's best wealth will be a few sheep with which he flees into the mountains."[41]

Now, I claim no special knowledge as to the timing of the last days; neither is it fully clear to me what the Muslim scriptures envisage. Yet these recurrent Prophetic teachings about a time when greed is not only widespread but also trumpeted as a virtue and when force seems merely to add to the turbulence must figure in any Muslim debate about the present reality of our world. Bin-Ladenism, with its fury against global imbalance, is unveiled as simply another manner of being Western, as John Gray has calculated.[42] If world trade is currently iniquitous, attacking the World Trade Center is no less iniquitous, like growing a rank weed in the same fetid soil of greed, envy, and lack of compassion.

Must the conclusion, then, be that things, duly subject to the divine rigor, are broadly as they should be? Is Islam, in the end, this fatalistic? Should we accept that the only way of seeing the world is in terms of spiritual worth and salvation, so that Ishmael, that third monotheism whose home is the "third world," must never aspire to the privileges of power and wealth enjoyed by the followers of the established religions of the Anglosphere? Should we sit back as Jerusalem is reconquered by Isaac, to be made a city of the wealthy, where Ishmael is progressively shut out of sight, his hovels bulldozed away, and while Mecca remains the resort of the poor, their greatest gathering place on earth?[43] Has the divine rigor decreed that the two cities shall be icons of the present global polarity?

Like all attempts to make the world and history religiously tidy, this vision of a God of the Ishmaelite ghetto is not so easy to sustain. There are wealthy Muslims, particularly in the oil-rich states: Are we to consider them heirs to the covenant of Isaac simply because, for instance, the Saudi princes are fêted at the Halliburton headquarters and in the Bible-believing White House? The Gulf region is developing a kind of prosperity Qur'ān no less peculiar than the prosperity gospel that drives many American right-wing voters; and there is a reading of Ibn Taymiya that makes this at least theoretically feasible.[44] It seems that despite the starvation that afflicts much of our world, there may be as many who speak of an ethic of feasting in Islam as in Christianity.

Perhaps we are being overly simple in our understanding of the two sons. The complexity of the scriptural accounts should mean that our generalizations will always be vulnerable. Rather than using, as they often do, current global inequalities as proof of Isaac's unworthiness, Muslims need to recognize that Christianity also exists massively in the developing world and shares much of

Ishmael's deprivation and desire for greater opportunity and respect. When the archbishop of Vienna speaks in favor of Zionism, the Palestinian clergy who oppose him are, we may say, Ishmaelites by allegiance as well as by descent.[45] While we may not go as far as Westermann, who, taxed by the Genesis sibling-rivalry tale, tries to see Ishmael as a kind of archetype of Christ, there is clearly a "poor-Christianity," perhaps we could even say an Ebionite one, that Muslims must legitimately recognize as Ishmaelite in spirit.[46] The community of James was, in a way, Ishmaelite, cast out into the Arabian desert, committed to a faith-plus-works theology, and although historical speculation on a possible Ebionite ancestry for Islam seems hard to support, the resemblance has been clear to not a few.[47] Muslims might want to see a Zealot-cum-Ebionite streak in some of the most impressive forms of English Christian socialism, for instance, or even, for the bolder hearted, in the liberation theology of the likes of Camillo Torres.[48]

The Gospels and the Sīra are not commensurable, and the revolutionary work of the Prophet has been echoed only obliquely by the liberation theologians, often with reference to Moses, that other great politician/emigrant for God, *muhājir*.[49] Yet the present revolutionary project in the Islamic world, which seeks to replace the alienated with the authentic, has not borne much fruit; it is stymied by the violence of the regimes or by its own abuses of power once established. If Christianity has moved toward a liberation theology, and Islam is, at least in its majoritarian formulations, gaining in skepticism about the current viability of linking the nation-state entirely to a rigorist form of sacred law, then perhaps there is a real convergence in aims and vision against the global corporate monoculture of greed.[50] Here is an opportunity to court unpopularity together, to offer a radical way of valuing poverty, while being counted, as Christians and Muslims equally, among those who riot for bread.

Speaking to the Heart

꿍

Ellen F. Davis

I begin this essay by stating the assumption that justifies its place in our program, namely that the ecological crisis is in the first instance not a technological crisis but a theological one. It is a crisis that concerns us precisely as creatures before their creator—the only creature, as far as we know, who is sensible of being obligated to a creator. But then, we are the only creature who needs to be sensible of that obligation, as we are the only one capable of failing in it. It is just within the last few years that the church has begun to recognize the ecological crisis for what it is: the most far-reaching crisis in our life with God. Yet that understanding has its roots already in scripture. In this essay I suggest how we may read our current situation in light of the Bible, and especially the prophets.

The prophets are perhaps the single best biblical resource for addressing our current situation—first of all because they speak, more directly and fully than any other biblical writers, to the human faculty that they call *lev*, "heart." To use nonmetaphorical and therefore less capacious language, they try to arouse in their hearers the will to change. And that is what is at stake: We are challenged, more widely and profoundly than any previous generation of humans, to change. As terrestrial ecologist Peter Vitousek has expressed it, now for the first time the human species as a whole must find the will to make a drastic change in our behavior so that life on this planet may continue to be viable and to some degree lovely.[51] As religious people, we might say "praiseworthy," recognizably the reason to offer praise to God, and it is well to remember that from a biblical perspective humans are not the only creatures who regularly offer up their praises.

A second and related reason for turning to the prophets: They enable us to see the present moment of history in divine perspective. The oldest Hebrew word for "prophet" is *hozeh*, or "seer." Prophets see the world as God sees it, with a wide-angle lens, so that the whole stretch, from creation to the end of days, is visible at once. Further, the prophets see God's involvement in history, and they speak for God in the midst of the flux of history. Although the prophets often express their own deep anguish, they speak for God clearly, without confusion. They look squarely at the worst, without obfuscation. Listen to Jeremiah, from the fourth chapter, speaking now for God:

> [Thus says the Lord:]
> My people are stupid;
> me, they know not.
> They are foolish children;
> they are not discerning.
> They are wise in doing evil,
> but good, they do not know how to do.[52]

Jeremiah begins by articulating God's first-person perspective. And then, without pause or even a change in beat, the prophet recounts what he has "seen":

> I have seen the earth, and here, [it is] without form and void (*tohu vavohu*);
> and [I look] to the heavens—and their light is gone.
> I have seen the mountains, and here, they are rocking,
> and all the hills palpitate.
> I have seen, and here, there is no human being,
> and all the birds of the heavens have fled.
> I have seen, and here, the garden-land is now the wasteland,
> and all its cities are pulled down,
> because of YHWH,[53] because of his hot anger. (Jer. 4:23–26)

Ra'iti, "I have seen" is repeated four times here. Jeremiah is teaching us to see just as he does, to look with unblinkered eyes on the undoing of creation: "*Ra'iti 'et ha'aretz*—I have seen the earth,[54] and look, it is formless and waste, *tohu vavohu*."[55] That memorable language of chaos appears uniquely here and in the first chapter of Genesis. Jeremiah takes us directly back to the first moments of the world and leads us stage by stage through the horrible inversion of creation. The first thing to go, of course, is the light. Then the mountains, the solid framework on which all else rests, are destabilized. Then the birds disappear, the creatures that God made and blessed on the fifth day and told them, "Be fruitful and multiply" (Gen. 1:22). Once they are eliminated, then it is inevitable that the creatures of the sixth day will likewise disappear: "There is no human being, *eyn 'adam.*" The humans whom God first charged to till the garden disappear, so garden-land reverts to wasteland, and the cities collapse. I live in a country in which farming is the most rapidly disintegrating sector of our national economy. In the Great Plains, traditionally known as the "heart-land"—although, tellingly, we now often refer to them as the "fly-over states" —many rural towns that were viable and modestly prosperous fifty years ago have become ghost towns. "I have seen, and look, the garden-land is now the wasteland, and all its cities are pulled down."

"I have seen the mountains, and here they are, rocking, and all the hills palpitate." It was Jeremiah's vision of de-creation that came into my mind in summer 1996, when I visited what is called in my country a "mountaintop removal site." In West Virginia and Kentucky, wherever it is no longer suffi-ciently profitable to extract coal by deep mining, it has now become common practice to blow the mountain away, literally—to reduce it to rubble, layer by layer, and take out the thin veins of coal. The rest is left as piles of infertile rock, over which the thinnest coating of grass has been spread, like pancake makeup on a ravaged face. Those mountains of the region we call Appalachia are, geologically speaking, the oldest part of the North American continent, the place where God began work on our quadrant of the globe. In this generation we are, as Jeremiah saw, undoing the good work that God did, returning it to absolute chaos, *tohu vavohu.*

So, did Jeremiah prophesy mountaintop removal, that particular form of human evil that would occur some 2,600 years after his own time? Not exactly. The form of chaos that Jeremiah immediately envisioned was the catastrophic destruction of Jerusalem—threatened several times, and probably by more than one great power, during Jeremiah's long career and finally accomplished by the Babylonians in 587–86 BCE. Yet, in G. B. Caird's words, "The prophets looked to the future with bifocal vision. With their near sight they foresaw imminent historical events which would be brought about by familiar human causes. . . . With their long sight they saw the day of the Lord" (a day of final reckoning), and they frequently "impose[d] the one image on the other," using the same language for both.[56] We are located now somewhere between the events the prophets immediately anticipated or confronted and the day of the Lord, and it is not our place to judge precisely where we are on that continuum. Nonetheless, we may take from the prophet a verbal image that enables us to comprehend the nature and magnitude of the evil we face, which we ourselves have wrought. Jeremiah gives us language, as the biblical prophets so often do, that breaks through what Walter Brueggemann so aptly calls "our achieved satiation," the numbness carefully wrought by my own national culture and so far successfully maintained for the voting majority of its citizens.[57] Prophetic speech is the antidote to the illness from which we are not eager to recover, namely apathy—the inability to feel shock, horror, and remorse for our actions.[58]

Jeremiah has been called "the poet of the land par excellence."[59] Through his eyes, we see the specific features of a tormented land:

> Over the mountains I raise a weeping and wailing,
> and over the pastures of the wilderness a lament. (Jer. 9:8)

That prophetic lamentation over the mountains and their pastures is especially poignant when spoken in this lovely land of Bosnia-Herzegovina, where war has left villages bereft of people and flocks, where clear-cutting of hardwood forests and damming of streams and rivers have reached critical proportions.[60] Jeremiah's outcry is strikingly appropriate: "If only my head were made of water and my eyes were a fountain of tears!" (Jer. 8:23). How can you ever grieve enough for the destruction of creation and human culture?

It is because genuine prophetic speech aims at destroying apathy that, as the Bible shows, the state and those in power almost always view such speech as a threat to their interests. Consider the effect when this statement—"the garden-land is now the wasteland"—is put in larger biblical perspective, juxtaposed with other strong statements about the fertile land and human effects on it. I have already suggested that Jeremiah is witnessing to the neglect of the original and still primary human vocation; he expects us to recall that in the second chapter of the Bible, the first humans were set in the garden to work its fertile soil, *le'ovdah uleshomrah*, "to serve it and to preserve it" (Gen. 2:15). Even more telling is the connection with Psalm 72, a royal psalm associated with Solomon. It begins with a prayer for just rule: "Give the king your justice, O God." It might be observed that the very fact of praying for a just king suggests the possibility or likelihood that empire will be built up through injustice—a suspicion that is confirmed by the biblical accounts of almost all the kings, Solomon included. Particularly interesting for our purposes is the fact that the psalmist's picture of a justly governed people encompasses the land as well:

> May there be an abundance of grain in the land [*or*: on the earth],[61]
> at the top of the mountains
> may its fruit wave (*yir'ash*) like the Lebanon. (Ps. 72:16)

Ra'ash, "wave"—it is exactly the same word that Jeremiah applies to the mountains.[62] While the psalmist sees the covering of grain waving on the mountaintops, Jeremiah sees the mountains themselves wavering (*ro'ashim*) and collapsing before God's hot anger. The coincidence of the word underscores the fact that their visions are diametrically opposed. When Jeremiah sees the fruitful land become barren, it is a sure sign that there is no justice in the seat of power.

The prophetic attack on apathy targets our strange and dangerous inability to be astonished. Through the media, we are regularly confronted with news that is by any measure astonishing. Here I use that word *news* in the strong sense, because no previous generation has heard or seen news reports like those we encounter: for instance, the report published by the Royal Society in March, stating that "two-thirds of the natural machinery that supports life on Earth is being degraded by human pressure."[63] The single bit of news I most vividly recall was a front-page photo taken at the North Pole in high summer 2000, from the deck of a Russian icebreaker. However, the ship had reached its destination without breaking any ice; it was clear, open water at the North Pole. An oceanographer on the icebreaker said that this was a sight that presumably no human being had ever seen. "The last time scientists can be certain the pole was awash in water was more than 50 million years ago."[64]

Why, then, are we not astonished at what we hear and see?[65] The biblically informed answer is that we lack the imagination to be astonished. I began by saying that the prophets speak to the *lev*, the heart. The theologian Garrett Green suggests that "imagination" may be in contemporary idiom the single best concept by which to express all that the biblical writers imply with the word *heart*.[66] Often prophets speak *of* and *to* the diseased imagination: "The heart is more perverse than anything, and it is sick" (Jer. 17:9). Their aim is to restore its proper function, and often that function is to assess the depth, scope, and causes of the tragedies that grip our world. The prophets aim to restore "the tragic imagination," which, paradoxically, is essential to the health and ultimately the survival of any community, precisely because it is the faculty whereby we reckon with devastating loss. As the contemporary agrarian writer Wendell Berry points out, it is "the tragic imagination that, through communal form or ceremony, permits great loss to be recognized, suffered, and borne, and that makes possible some sort of consolation and renewal." In the end, then, after and through suffering, the tragic imagination enables "the return to the beloved community, or to the possibility of one."[67]

The tragic imagination reaches back into memory to recall the beloved community to itself. That is why poetry is one of the preeminent forms of imaginative expression, because it is the richest fruit of shared memory. As has long been observed, the biblical prophets were mostly poets. Their call to prophesy represents a point in history when God's memory and God's vision are given full human expression for the sake of a community's survival. The poet works by evoking not only past events but also past voices and "recalling [them] to presence" with a few resonant words.[68] The biblical poets often use that technique of resonance in order to disclose the depth of present experience.

One of the most powerful instances of such resonance is this passage from Isaiah:

> Look, YHWH empties the earth and devastates it,
> and he distorts its face and scatters its inhabitants. . . .
> The earth withers, it wastes;
> the world languishes, lies waste.
> The exalted of the earth's people languish,
> and the earth is polluted beneath its inhabitants,
> for they have transgressed teachings (*torot*),
> altered decrees, and violated an everlasting covenant.
> Therefore a curse devours the earth,
> and those who live on it are guilty.
> Therefore the inhabitants of the earth are seared,[69]
> and few humans are left. (Isa. 24:1, 4–6)

The earth that humans were meant to serve and preserve now lies "polluted beneath its inhabitants"; we have distorted the order of creation, transgressed

[divine] teachings, altered decrees, "violated *brit 'olam*, an everlasting covenant." That last phrase clarifies the prophet's intention. The first time it appears
is in the early chapters of Genesis, when after the flood God sets his bow in the
heavens, as a sign of a unilateral disarmament treaty, a *brit 'olam* between God
"and every living being, among all flesh that is on the earth."[70] Now when
Isaiah says, "They have violated an everlasting covenant," he is making the
stunning claim that humans have broken God's unilateral treaty *from their side*.
Against all logic and self-interest, they—we—have thrown back into God's face
the divine promise never again to bring destruction upon the earth:

> And YHWH breathed in the savoury scent [of Noah's sacrifice], and YHWH
>   said, "I will not again curse the fertile soil on account of the human being
>   . . . and I will not again strike down every living being as I have done.
> All the days of the earth, seed and harvest and cold and heat
> and summer and winter and day and night—they will cease no more." (Gen.
>   8:21–22)

In two poetic lines, the biblical writer sums up all that we take for granted
about the stability of our climate. It informs us that what we have heretofore
assumed to be a "built-in" feature of the world is rather, in a world disordered
by human sin, a mark of divine forbearance, an expression of God's covenantal
faithfulness. If we are now beginning to experience significant disruption of
climatic patterns, then the divine promise exposes the hollowness of claims
(ironically, often maintained by "Bible-believing Christians") that this is nothing more than natural fluctuation.[71] A more discerning reading of the Bible
leads us to apply to ourselves Isaiah's telling diagnosis: "They have violated an
everlasting covenant."

Our situation, then, is one of complete vulnerability. We have brought
that vulnerability upon ourselves through our persistent refusal to heed the
limits that God did indeed build into the created order, a refusal that the
Bible dates back to the first human couple. "They have transgressed [divine]
teachings"—our willful violation has returned the earth to its condition *before*
God's covenant with Noah, a condition that Genesis describes with one word:
hamas, "violence" (Gen. 6:11, 13). So the end of Isaiah's oracle portrays the
sluice gates of heaven opening again, as they did in Noah's time. The foundations of the earth "totter," then "crumble"; "it falls and does not rise again"
(Isa. 24:20; cf. Amos 5:2).

Isaiah, like Jeremiah, withholds from us ready assurances about the future of humankind and even of the earth itself. Neither suggests that the earth as we know it is a permanent part of the created order. In short, the prophetic witness deprives us of the self-assurance that is always the fruit of bad faith. Yet at the same time that they strip us of that encumbrance, the prophets also supply us with a deeper understanding of what form *good* faith must take in our currently deteriorating situation. Both Jeremiah and Isaiah confront us with the reality of our creatureliness, and specifically with the following two related facts.

First, creation is bound into a single, covenanted unity. Each of us is connected to every other creature by the great web of life that the biblical writers call *brit 'olam*, an everlasting covenant. Therefore our charity and our sense of responsibility cannot be selective. Wendell Berry comments aptly on the Bible's "elaborate understanding of charity": "Once begun, wherever it begins, it cannot stop until it includes all creation, for all creatures are parts of a whole upon which each is dependent, and it is a contradiction to love your neighbour and despise the great inheritance on which his life depends."[72]

Second, like every other member of this covenanted unity, we humans occupy a place that is delimited by divine *torot*, teachings, and when we violate the prescribed limits, the consequences are inevitably disastrous, for ourselves, for "all flesh," and for the earth itself.

So in concrete terms, good faith means living as the creatures we are, consciously and willingly manifesting our creatureliness in our actions. The forms of meaningful creaturely action, as modeled by the prophets themselves, include prayer—intercessory and healing prayer—and various forms of symbolic action. In my own cultural context, various forms of self-denial are perhaps the most appropriate form of symbolic action, and our asceticism should probably begin with our supermarkets and our garages. Meaningful creaturely action extends also to political involvement, to far-reaching economic and social practices that bespeak a realistic hope in the God who, even now, is known to us as the One who "creates [present-tense verb] the heavens and forms the earth."[73] So Isaiah says, and he adds, "Not as waste (*tohu*) has he created it; for habitation he has formed it" (Isa. 45:18). All that is required of us, as creatures, is to live in accordance with that divine intention. ·

Āyatology and Raḥmatology

Islam and the Environment

ဢ

Aref Ali Nayed

It is difficult to know where to begin in discussing "Islam and the environment"; writing and reflection on this theme have, to date, been very scarce.[74] This seems to me to demonstrate something of a crisis in contemporary Muslim theology; in light of this, I propose to examine the preconditions of a Muslim theology of the environment rather than to give citations from the Qur'ān and the Sunna in an attempt to show that Islam is as profound on this question as the latest books on ecology. The latter approach, where people will seek to find verses from the Qur'ān or Sunna that validate the latest ecological theory, is common, but it seems to me that that kind of theology, while it may be good apologetics, is neither deep nor useful.

Muslim theology was at one point a great edifice of writings, from which we still benefit today; it was the articulation from generation to generation of what Muslims believed most deeply. During the 'Abbāsid period, even as late as the Ottoman period, theologians worked carefully to articulate their faith (*imān*). Unfortunately, there has been a certain stagnation in this area more recently; it is problematic that nobody of the stature of al-Ghazālī, al-Ash'arī, or al-Māturīdī has been produced lately. It seems to me that many of the problems experienced by Muslim communities today are linked to bad preaching, which can in turn be traced to bad, inadequate, or weak theology. I believe that many of our problems cannot be addressed only by political or social or economic means; they require deep and critical self-reflection at a theological level. The question I pose is this: What fundamental notions have we lost sight of, the absence of which has led to a poor theology of the environment?[75]

There are notions in the Qur'an that are very important to invoke and that have been invoked in recent writing on the environment, such as *iṣlaḥ*, "mending," and its opposite, *fasad* or *ifsad*, the "corruption" of the earth, or the "balance," *mīzān*, spoken of in the Qur'ān, and the disturbing of this balance. These are important notions deserving much further reflection. However, I would rather focus on two other realities. The first is *āya*, "sign," and the second is *raḥma*, "compassion." I propose to explore how the rehabilitation of *āyāt* and *raḥma* can help us to derive a Muslim theology of the environment that is sustaining for our preaching and so can lead to improved conditions in our environment. Muslim countries today are among the most polluted in the world; where they are not polluted is only due to a lack of industrialization of development, and when industrialization does take place, they become extremely polluted. My own country of Libya is an example of this. In the 1960s, before development took place, the environment was wonderful, but this was destroyed in the 1970s by the building of cement factories that have blighted the coastline and depleted the water table. Problems of this kind in our praxis surely point to something wrong with our theology—not with our religion (*dīn*) as such, for this is based on revelation (*waḥy*), but with our articulation and understanding of our faith.

Āyatology: A World of Signs

The word *āya* is repeated many times in the Qur'ān: The Qur'ān is indeed a cluster of *āyāt* that continually refer to *āyāt*.[76] This is often translated as (divine) "signs," yet the more one reads the Qur'ān the more one realizes that there is more to *ayāt* than signification in the sense of just "pointing to." *Āyāt* are dynamic, operative, transformative processes. I believe that one project necessary for the rehabilitation of Muslim theology today is the articulation of what we can call "*āyatology*," the science that studies divine indicative processes. Just as we have the "monadology" of Leibniz or the "phenomenology" of Husserl, so it should be possible to construct a science of "āyatology," informed not only by the Qur'an, the Sunna, and tradition but also by such fields as speech–act theory, pragmatics, semiotics, and hermeneutics.

What is this āyatology about? Āyatology is an Islamic theology that begins with Allah as *al-raḥman*, the source of all compassion, and is hence ultimately deeply related to "raḥmatology," the second dimension of theology discussed here. Allah's compassion is manifest dynamically, actively, and continuously in transformative processes that keep indicating him all the time. These processes are called *āyāt*; they can be seen as activities and sometimes as things. Āyatology as ontology attempts to offer typologies of *āyāt* and to describe how we can account for things, events, acts, and artifacts. *Āyāt* as divine indicative and transformative activities demand human engagement. This engagement is dynamic and dialogical. It is dialogical in that it is an active and mutually transformative exchange between the seer (being also himself or herself an *āya*) and the *āya* that he or she happens to be considering. It is also dialogical in the sense of engaging other human *āyāt* who are themselves seeking to engage the same *āya* or other similar *āyāt*. Āyatology attempts to offer typologies of modes of *āya* engagement and how they work.

I have given a general summary of what āyatology is about, but let me try to express this in simpler terms. One of the most important and devastating factors that has led to the lack of a theology of the environment in Islam is that we have adopted the modern way of looking at things as mere things. This has been the source of many of our problems; even when we wish to develop a theology of the environment, we presuppose that the environment is a cluster of things—although we may say that it is a balanced or an elegantly built cluster of things. Once you assume the "thingliness" of the environment, you have already lost the necessary presupposition; you cannot produce a Muslim theology of the environment if you look at things as mere things.

So we must rehabilitate our ability to see "things" as *āyāt*, so that when we look at things we are aware of their indicative, transformative divine source and also their destination. When you look at a tree, for example, you should be seeing through its trace (*athar*) the divine *fāʿil*, the act of creation. Through the *fāʿil*, you should be able to ascend to the divine *ism*, "name," which has brought forth this activity. Through the divine name, you would reach the corresponding divine *ṣifa*, "attribute," and from the *ṣifa* the divine essence, *dhāt*. This sequence of trace-act-name-attribute-essence means that everything that is seen in the world is seen as a gateway to Allah, a way to commune with, be in the presence of, and worship him. If we only see things in themselves as things, we are basically looking at the door as a wall; we are not opening the door to go farther. Once this foundational point is missed, all is lost. Even ibn ʿAṭāʾ Allāh al-Iskandarī, the great Mālikī scholar and Shādhilī sheikh, says,

"When the beginnings are luminescent, the ends are also luminescent." When we begin with things as things, we lose track and can end up only with things. No matter how much we say or think about the environment, if we look at trees, stones, animals, human beings in this way, there is no way out of the lock of the thingliness of things.

The rehabilitation of a discourse on *āyāt* is a huge challenge, because in Islamic history the *āyāt* have been forgotten in favor of notions such as *wujūd*, "being." In early Muslim theology, there is scarcely any talk of *wujūd*, but when the philosophers arrive, the *to on* of the Greeks replaces the *āyāt*. The process can be traced through al-Juwaynī, al-Ghazālī and al-Rāzī to al-Taftazānī until in the Ottoman theologians the emphasis is entirely on *wujūd*. This is the case also in the Shī'ī tradition, where for Mulla Ṣadra *wujūd* is the start of the whole discourse. I believe that to begin in this way with "being" leads to a tendency toward "thingliness" in approach. It is imperative to begin with something more divine and more basic than being. This sounds strange, as we normally think of ontology as most fundamental, yet I believe that *raḥma*, "compassion," is more fundamental than being.

Raḥmatology: A World Manifesting Divine Compassion

If we read the Qur'ān and Sunna carefully, we find that being as such is only a manifestation of divine *raḥma*. Being itself is a gift, and that gift is because of a tendency to gift, *al-raḥmaniyya*, which is Allah himself. Thus there is a direct link between *raḥma* and *āya*, between raḥmatology and āyatology. *Āyāt* are intrinsically related to *raḥma* because if it were not for God's compassion toward us he would not have shown us things—*āyāt* are ultimately a kind of showing, a transformative showing that changes us. This is a showing that can be taken into the heart, leading to transformation from the inside. This transformative showing is a divine compassion, so that when you are looking at the tree you can receive a manifestation of *raḥma* of sorts. Of course, if you see things in this way it will be impossible simply to destroy the tree in the name of technological exploitation.

For Muslims, this āyatology is definitely normative. Allah did not leave us to our whims when it comes to engaging the *āyāt*. On the contrary, he gave us plenty of advice on this subject. The Qur'ān is remarkable in being a set of *āyāt* that tells us how to deal with *āyāt*. It is not possible here to give an account of all the Qur'ānic guidance in this matter, but one or two points may be emphasized. Primarily, there is a divine promise that those who are arrogant will not see the *āyāt*; the first rule in āyatology must be the invocation of humility, of a feeling of poverty before Allah and before his creatures. The creation should be seen in a sense as a set of teachers: ibn al-'Arabī, for example, describes how, walking past a gutter, he came to the realization: "One of my masters is a gutter." He has seen how the gutter gathered the waters and put them in one place, and so he learned how to focus. In this case, even something manufactured could be seen as a teacher.

This attitude of humility does not fit well with the "thingliness" attitude that we normally have. One of the most devastating occurrences in Muslim history was when, under pressure from colonialism and the scientific thinking of the West, many Islamic scholars began to develop a kind of scientistic theology. In an attempt to escape from a misty mysticism, a very positivistic Kant-like theology was developed: *Islām dīn al-'ilm*, "Islam is the religion of knowledge," where *'ilm* ("knowledge") is here taken as equivalent to "science." *'Ilm* traditionally, however, included such elements as humility; as Imām Mālik said, "*'Ilm* is a light that is thrown into the heart." As *'ilm* came to be thought of as "science," so *āyāt* came to be thought of as "things." There was indeed historical precedence for this in Muslim history through the introduction from Greek thought of the idea of *wujūd*, "being." By the time of al-'Afghānī and 'Abduh, this results in theologies that are quite scientistic in their assumptions and that include few references to *āyāt*.

To return to the Qur'ānic teaching: The first point is the need to be free of *istikbar*, the belief that I am bigger than the *āya*, that I am the subject and it is the object, that I am its conqueror, that I am the doer and the *āya* the done-to. I must learn to stand in humility before the *āya*. The second Qur'ānic rule is the imperative to respond to the *āyāt*. I must respond by recognizing that the *āyāt*, all the things that surround me, are gifts. Amid such gifts, I must make the response of *shukr*, "gratitude" or "thanks." *Shukr* is so important in Islam that in several *āyāt* it is equated with Islam itself; infidelity, *kufr*, is the opposite of gratitude. If we are not grateful for that which we receive, we are committing a crime against Allah. The destruction of gifts is in fact called *kufr*, an infidelity involving rejection or covering up of gifts. The response of gratitude involves not destroying them, and it also requires that we share them so that we can spread them. Moreover, if one of the gifts is in some sense breaking down, it must be repaired—this *islah* becomes a form of *shukr*; equally and oppositely, *ifsad*, "destruction," becomes a form of *kufr*.

The Qur'ān therefore teaches the ethics of humility and of gratitude in relation to the *āyāt*. It is very interesting to see that within the Qur'ān's presentation of the *āyāt* there is no clear delineation between us and the environment. We are ourselves *āyāt*, and the environment is a set of *āyāt*. The prophets also are *āyāt*, and the books of God are *āyāt*. The natural processes we see, such as the alternation of night and day, are *āyāt*; the miracles of the prophets are also *āyāt*. Within this ocean of *āyāt* it is possible to develop some typologies. For example, on the one hand there are the *āyāt* of the horizons, and on the other hand the *āyāt* of the inward. There are great *āyāt* and there are small *āyāt*, and so on. Despite the development of such typologies, the Qur'ān clearly presents the *āyāt* as a continuum; there is no severance between the human being and the environment. Thus it is not right to speak of "us and the environment." Rather, we *are* the environment; we are each other's environment, we are an environment to our own environment, and our environment is an environment to us. Any severance between us and the environment, any language of doing things to the environment, even of preserving the environment as an object, is problematic according to a Qur'ānic āyatology.

Responding to *Āya* and *Raḥma*

People's reactions to the *āyāt* differ. Those who take the *āyāt* in the right way in the Qur'ān are described as those who ask, those who believe, those who understand, grasp, or know, those who are alert. This is a kind of awareness, rather like the "seeing" of the Hebrew Bible; it is also a kind of waiting, acceptance, patience, or humility. The opposite attitude is that of not hearing, not caring, ignoring, being arrogant, having a stony heart toward the *āyāt*. The Qur'ān describes this also in terms of not bowing before the Qur'ān, as in several places where the *āyāt* of Allah are presented, people fall down before them, so great is their reverence. This reverence arises because people do not see the things in themselves but see Allah through the *āyāt*, through the sequence of trace-act-name-attribute-essence described before. Although the divine essence can be seen by nobody, this provides a trajectory leading toward it, so that the *āya* becomes a gateway rather than a wall, an opening rather than a closure. Thus those who take all things around them with the right attitude as *āyāt* are on the way to salvation; those who take them with another attitude as things lead themselves, and others, to destruction. This is the clear teaching of the Qur'ān.

The second key dimension required for a Muslim theology of the environment is that of *raḥma*. As explained earlier, the very manifestation of *āyāt*, the fact that we are granted *āyāt*, is because of Allah's *raḥma*. It is surprising, if one looks at the treatment of the *ṣifāt* by al-Ash'arī or al-Maturīdī, the founders of the two orthodox schools of Sunni theology, to see the conspicuous absence of the *āyāt*. This absence is for historical reasons rather than for any spiritual reason; even al-Bāqillānī speaks of *lutf*, "grace," and in ibn al-'Arabī there is a huge discourse on *raḥma*. In listing the twenty *ṣifāt* recognized in the creed, though, there is little reference to the names *al-raḥman* or *al-raḥīm*. *Raḥma* is not emphasized; rather, emphasis is placed on *irāda*, "will," and *'ilm*, "knowledge."

This seems to me to be problematic in our time. In the days of al-Ash'arī and al-Maturīdī, the centrality of *raḥma* was so well known that it did not need to be articulated. They drank, as it were, of *raḥma* in their daily water and their daily meals, and their societies were in many ways quite compassionate. Moreover, this continued until recent times—the ways in which communities in North Africa would deal with each other in the 1960s and 1970s, for example, was far from the greed, cruelty, and individualism we see today. We seem to have lost a sense of mutual compassion, and in light of this loss it is now time to rearticulate the centrality of *raḥma*. The great theologians of the past were not uncompassionate people; indeed, many of them were great Sufis and spiritual masters. However, this has been forgotten or neglected today, partly because of a discourse coming from scientism.[77]

In this way, I believe that the lack of discourse on *raḥma*, and the lack of practice of *raḥma*, have led us into crisis. The abundance of cruelty that we see around us in so many societies today is by no means restricted to the Islamic world, but if we can recover the sense of the environment as a set of *āyāt*, teeming, puzzling, and marvelous activities of God springing from his *raḥma*, then we can rehabilitate an Islamic theology that will help us out of the crisis we face.

Notes

1. Leviticus 25:8–17.
2. Jasna Šamić, *Dîvân de Kâ'imî: vie et oeuvre d'un poète bosniaque du XVIIe siècle* (Paris: Recherche sur les Civilisations, 1986), 28–35.
3. Clifford Geertz, *Islam Observed: Religious Development in Morocco and Indonesia* (New Haven, CT: Yale University Press, 1968), 34.
4. Yaḥyā al-Nawawī, *Sharḥ al-Arba'īn*, trans. Louis Pouzet, *Une Herméneutique de la tradition islamique: Le commentaire des Arba'ūn al-Nawawīya de Muḥyi' al-Dīn Yaḥyā al-Nawawī (m. 676/1277)* (Beirut: Dar el-Mashreq, 1982), 167.
5. Jalāl al-Dīn Rūmī, *Mathnawī*, trans. Reynold A. Nicholson (London: Luzac, 1925–40), 2:403.
6. Bukhārī and Muslim.
7. These hadiths are cited in Muḥammad 'Alawī al-Mālikī, *Muḥammad al-Insān al-Kāmil* (Jeddah: Dār al-Shurūq, 1404/1984), 156–68.
8. Sharaf al-Dīn al-Būṣīrī, *Burdat al-madīḥ*, in Ibn Ḥajar al-Haytamī, *al-'Umda fī sharḥ al-Burda* (Dubai: Dār al-Faqīh, 1424/2003), 201.
9. In al-Haytamī, *al-'Umda fī sharḥ al-Burda*, 205.
10. For these, see Adam Sabra, *Poverty and Charity in Medieval Islam: Mamluk Egypt, 1250–1517* (Cambridge: Cambridge University Press, 2000), 8–31.
11. In al-Haytamī, *Al-'Umda fī sharḥ al-Burda*, 208.
12. For the relevant material here, see Abū Ḥāmid al-Ghazālī, *Iḥyā' 'Ulūm al-Dīn* (Cairo: Muṣṭafā al-Ḥalabī, 1347), 2:338–39.
13. William C. Chittick, *The Sufi Path of Love: The Spiritual Teaching of Rumi* (Albany: State University of New York Press, 1983), 186–91.
14. The best known is Jalāl al-Dīn al-Suyūṭī (d. 1505), *Kifayat al-ṭālib al-labīb fī khaṣā'is al-ḥabīb* (Hyderabad: Dā'irat al-Mā'arif al-Nimīya, 1319–20/1901–2); the work is conventionally known as *al-Khaṣā'iṣ al-Kubrā.*
15. Ghazālī, *Iḥyā' 'Ulūm al-Dīn*, 4:167; the hadith is narrated by Tirmidhī.
16. Ibid., 4:171; hadith is in Ibn Mājah's collection.
17. Ibid., 4:189.
18. Ibid., 3:82–85. Another representative opinion: "*Zuhd* is not at all identical with abandoning the search for a living, as some imagine who go to such extremes that they resemble the Manicheans, the Brahmins and the monks; for that would lead to the ruin of the world." al-Rāghib al-Iṣfahānī, *al-Dharī'a ilā makārim al-Sharī'a* (Beirut: Dār al-Jīl, 1400/1980), 215.

19. Tirmidhī, Zuhd, 3.

20. Šamić, Dîvân de Kâ'imî, 87.

21. Ibid., 132.

22. The best English anthology of Muslim logia attributed to him is Tarif Khalidi, *The Muslim Jesus: Sayings and Stories in Islamic Literature* (Cambridge, MA: Harvard University Press, 2001).

23. Šamić, Dîvân de Kâ'imî, 88.

24. Colin Davis, *Levinas: An Introduction* (Cambridge: Polity, 1996), 94; see also Vincenzo Vitiello, "Desert, Ethos, Abandonment: Towards a Topology of the Religious," in *Religion,* ed. Jacques Derrida and Gianni Vattimo (Cambridge: Polity, 1998), 147–48.

25. Emmanuel Levinas, trans. Seán Hand, *Difficult Freedom: Essays on Judaism* (London: Athlone, 1990), 140.

26. "When Simone Weil wrote: 'the proof that the content of Christianity pre-existed Christ is that there have been no great changes since in the behaviour of men,' we believe that the argument can be turned around." Levinas, *Difficult Freedom,* 137.

27. Ibid., 135.

28. Safet Bektović, "The Doubled Movement of Infinity in Kierkegaard and Sufism," *Islam and Christian-Muslim Relations* 10 (1999): 325–27.

29. Levinas, *Difficult Freedom,* 101.

30. For the texts, see Tim Winter, "The Last Trump Card: Islam and the Supersession of Other Faiths," *Studies in Interreligious Dialogue* 9 (1999): 144–45.

31. Ziauddin Ahmed, *Islam, Poverty, and Income Distribution* (Leicester: Islamic Foundation, 1991), 48, 81; Zainul Abedin Patel, *Small Kindnesses: An Islamic Viewpoint on the Cause and Solution to Global Poverty,* 2nd ed. (Nuneaton: Muslim Venture, 1410/1990), 35.

32. Muḥammad ibn 'Abdallāh al-Azraqī, ed. Rushdī al-Ṣāliḥ Malḥas, *Akhbār Makka wa-mā jā'a fihā min al-āthār* (Madrid: Dar al-Andalus, 197?), 1:64, 2:66.

33. C. Westermann, *Genesis 12–36* (London: SPCK, 1985), 344.

34. Jill Robbins, *Prodigal Son/Elder Brother: Interpretation and Alterity in Augustine, Petrarch, Kafka, Levinas* (Chicago: University of Chicago Press, 1991), 5.

35. Ibid.

36. For a good introduction, see Muhammad Hamidullah, *Muslim Conduct of State* (Lahore: M. Ashraf, 1945), passim; S. A. Siddiqi, *Public Finance in Islam* (Lahore: M. Ashraf, 1948).

37. Sabra, *Poverty and Charity,* 69–100; Ahmad Issa Bey, *Histoire des bimaristans (hôpitaux) a l'époque islamique* (Cairo: P. Barbey, 1928).
38. Bukhārī, Fitan, 5; Muslim, 'Ilm, 11.
39. Muḥammad ibn Aḥmad al-Qurṭubī, *al-Tadhkira fi aḥwāl al-mawtā wa-umūr al-ākhira* (Cairo: al-Khānjī, 1352), 548.
40. Abū Dāūd, Fitan, 2.
41. Bukhārī, Fitan, 14; Riqāq, 34.
42. John Gray, *Al Qaeda and What It Means to Be Modern* (London: Faber and Faber, 2003), e.g., 1–2: "No cliché is more stupefying than that which describes Al Qaeda as a throwback to medieval times. It is a by-product of globalisation. Its most distinctive feature—projecting a privatised form of organised violence worldwide—was impossible in the past. Equally, the belief that a new world can be hastened by spectacular acts of destruction is nowhere found in medieval times. Al Qaeda's closest precursors are the revolutionary anarchists of late nineteenth-century Europe." Emulation of unbelievers is another sign of end-time decadence; see the hadith "You shall certainly follow the ways of the communities who came before you, inch for inch, and span for span, until even were they to crawl into a lizard-hole, you would follow them." al-Ḥākim al-Nīsābūrī, *al-Mustadrak 'ala'l-Ṣaḥīḥayn* (Hyderabad, 1334–42), 1:37.
43. One of Amos Oz's most disagreeable characters exclaims thus: "Why was Ishmael, the *goy,* called Ishmael which means: 'He shall hear the Lord'? Do you know? No? I will tell you. He was called Ishmael so that he could hear what Isaac, his brother and master, ordered him to do. And why was Isaac the Jew called Isaac: i.e., 'He shall laugh'? So that he could laugh at the sight—because the labor of righteous men is done by others." Amos Oz, *In the Land of Israel,* trans. M. Goldberg-Bartura (London: Chatto and Windus, 1983), 12.
44. Sabra, *Poverty and Charity,* 24–25. Ibn Taymīya is joined here by other "hard" Ḥanbalīs, such as Ibn al-Jawzī and Ibn al-Qayyim; the convergence between a strict scripturalism and a willingness to validate mercantile wealth presents interesting parallels with some Bible belt views. Cf. Simon Coleman, *The Globalisation of Charismatic Christianity: Spreading the Gospel of Prosperity* (Cambridge: Cambridge University Press, 2000).
45. "Papal Candidate Gives Pro-Zionist Talk," *Jerusalem Post,* March 31, 2005.
46. Westermann, *Genesis 12–36,* 344.

47. Such as Pierre-Antoine Bernheim, *James, Brother of Jesus* (London: SCM, 1997), 267; Robert Eisenman, *James, the Brother of Jesus* (London: Faber and Faber, 1997), 3.

48. Many Muslim stereotypes of a politically inert Christianity could be dispelled by a consideration of John Gerassi, ed., *Revolutionary Priest: The Complete Writings and Messages of Camillo Torres* (New York: Random House, 1971).

49. Annoyed by Christian political and social activism, the Japanese government in 1919 banned the book of Exodus—but not the Gospels. Bastiaan Wielenga, "Liberation Theology in Asia," in *The Cambridge Companion to Liberation Theology,* ed. Christopher Rowland (Cambridge: Cambridge University Press, 1999), 48. An interesting convergence of the two currently rival liberators, the Prophet Muhammad and George Washington, is suggested in rival applications of the book of Deuteronomy. The American patriot Timothy Dwight (1752–1817) spoke as follows of Deuteronomy 34:10–12: "Washington, like Moses, was born of simple, but worthy, parents; like Moses, he was trained in the wilderness; like Moses, he reluctantly answered God's call to serve his people." Cited in Clifford Longley, *Chosen People: The Big Idea That Shaped England and America* (London: Hodder and Stoughton, 2002), 141–42. Muslims have considered the passage in Deuteronomy 18:17–18 to be a foretelling of the Prophet, the new exodus leader and lawgiver. ʿAlī al-Ṭabarī, trans. A. Mingana, *The Book of Religion and Empire* (Manchester: University Press, Longmans, 1922), 85–86, 158.

50. An alternative to the radical Wahhābist agenda is offered by the major Islamic party of Indonesia, which was instrumental in bringing an end to a Western-backed dictatorship that had presided over extreme disparities of wealth. See Robert W. Hefner, *Civil Islam: Muslims and Democratization in Indonesia* (Princeton, NJ: Princeton University Press, 2000).

51. In a lecture at the Land Institute, Salina, Kansas, June 2003.

52. Jer. 4:22. All translations from the Bible are my own.

53. The letters *YHWH* are a transliteration of the Hebrew form of the name of God, traditionally viewed as too sacred to be pronounced. It is often rendered in English translations as "the Lord."

54. The word *ʿeretz* might be translated more narrowly ("land"), as it frequently is used with reference to the land of Israel. Jeremiah does have his own land of Judah particularly in mind, but because he is characterizing its collapse as a "global" disaster, I use the broader translation.

55. The second part of the phrase is not a real word but a rhyming syllable; "waste–schmaste" better captures the wordplay for English speakers.

56. George B. Caird, *The Language and Imagery of the Bible* (Grand Rapids, MI: Eerdmans, 1997), 258. Similarly, Brevard Childs notes the "trans-historical, apocalyptic colouring" of Jeremiah 4:23–26. In his view, an early oracle of Jeremiah has been expanded sometime after the fall of Jerusalem, and the language of chaos has been applied to that historical event. Brevard Childs, "The Enemy from the North and the Chaos Tradition," *Journal of Biblical Literature* 78 (1959): 187–98.

57. Walter Brueggemann, *The Prophetic Imagination* (Minneapolis, MN: Fortress Press: 1987), 45.

58. When I say (with Brueggemann) that prophetic speech is the antidote to apathy, I am indirectly citing the classic study of Abraham Joshua Heschel, who sees that what distinguishes the prophets from their con-temporaries is "a sympathy with divine pathos." *The Prophets: An Intro-duction* (New York: Harper & Row, 1962), 1:26.

59. Walter Brueggemann, *The Land* (Philadelphia, PA: Fortress Press, 1977), 107.

60. Tim Clancy, "The War on Bosnia," *World Watch* 17, no. 2 (2004): 12–23.

61. The Hebrew word is *'eretz*; see note 62.

62. Brevard Childs argues, "When we enter the Exilic and post-Exilic peri-ods, the eschatological usage of [*ra'ash*] in connection with the final judg-ment through a returned chaos is everywhere evident. In fact, it is our contention that the term has become a *terminus technicus* within the language of the return of chaos." "Enemy from the North," 189.

63. Tim Radford, "Two-thirds of World's Resources 'Used Up,'" *Guardian Unlimited,* March, 2005.

64. "Ages-Old Icecap at North Pole Is Now Liquid, Scientists Find," *New York Times*, Saturday, August 19, 2000, p. 1. The oceanographer cited is Dr. James J. McCarthy, director of the Museum of Comparative Zool-ogy at Harvard University and coleader of a group working for the UN-sponsored Intergovernmental Panel on Climate Change.

65. The question is, in a sense, obvious, yet I had not thought to ask it before reading the article by Ed Ayres, "Why Are We Not Astonished?" *World Watch* 12, no. 3 (1999): 24–29.

66. Garrett Green, *Imagining God: Theology and the Religious Imagination* (San Francisco: Harper & Row, 1989).

67. Wendell Berry, "Writer and Region," in *What Are People For?* (New York: North Point Press, 1990), 78.

68. Ibid., 89.

69. The meaning of the Hebrew verb is uncertain. Joseph Blenkinsopp offers evidence that might support another reading: "dwindle." See Joseph Blenkinsopp, *Isaiah 1–39*, Anchor Bible, vol. 19 (New York: Doubleday, 2000), 350.

70. Isa. 9:16. The phrase recurs in the account of the Abrahamic covenant (Gen. 17:7).

71. Cf. Michael Welker, *Creation and Reality* (Minneapolis, MN: Fortress Press, 1999), 37–38.

72. Wendell Berry, *The Gift of Good Land* (New York: North Point Press, 1981), 273.

73. On the importance of the biblical concept of "heavens and earth" for our understanding of creation, see Welker, *Creation and Reality*, 33–44.

74. This essay is reconstructed from an audio recording of the lecture given by Dr. Nayed at the Building Bridges seminar in Sarajevo.

75. To use the terminology of R. G. Collingwood, "absolute presuppositions."

76. The word *āyā* (pl. *āyāt*) refers not only to natural things in their capacity as signs (as developed by Dr. Nayed in this essay) but also to verses of the Qur'ān.

77. It is interesting to note in this regard how many Islamists are engineers. There seems to me a kind of engineering attitude in Islamism that can be very harmful for theology, as it leads to the attitude that you can just do things to things—including people among "things."

Conclusion
Building Bridges in Bosnia-Herzegovina

ℰ/๏

Michael Ipgrave

The image of "building a bridge" is in Bosnia-Herzegovina most powerfully associated with the beautiful Old Bridge in Mostar, which the seminar visited on its final day. Built across the Neretva River by the Ottoman architect Hajrudin in 1557, the bridge was famed throughout the region, praised by poets and painted by artists:

> This bridge was built as an arch of a rainbow
> Dear God, is there anything alike in the world?[1]

When the Old Bridge was destroyed in warfare in 1993, the general responsible is said to have responded with grim humor to those who remonstrated against the removal of this priceless heritage: "We will build a better bridge and an older one when we are finished." In 2004 the bridge was indeed reconstructed, a potent symbol of the rebuilding of the country and of the reconnection of its divided communities. Despite the fatuousness of the general's remark, his words can be taken as posing a challenge to all involved in building partnerships between Christians and Muslims today: Can we build bridges that are better than their predecessors and older? Better, in that they are more resilient in standing up to our testing times of division and enmity, and better also, in that they are more useful in serving the public good of communication.[2] Older, in the sense that the theological foundations for our relationships reach deeper into the historic cores of the Christian and the Muslim faiths.

In the Bosnian context, it became apparent at the seminar that there need to be three horizons in view for Muslims and Christians to be able to work together trustfully and positively in seeking a common ground. While the particular circumstances of Bosnia may bring these into a special salience, it seems clear that these three will apply to Christian–Muslim partnerships in any society. First, in relation to the past, there needs to be a purification of memory. The Second Vatican Council's "Declaration on the Relation of the Church to Non-Christian Religions" urged, in notably restrained terms: "Since in the course of centuries not a few quarrels and hostilities have arisen between Christians and Muslims, this sacred synod urges all to forget the past and to work sincerely for mutual understanding."[3] In a contested history such as that of Bosnia, where each community has suffered, it is tempting to be selective in what is remembered; it is easier to recall the sufferings that others have caused us than to admit what we have done to others. Yet new relationships can only be forged when the past is faced up to and acknowledgment made of guilt and complicity.

Second, looking to the present and the future, Christians and Muslims have to make a positive commitment to protect one another and communities of all faith in times of stress that lead to suspicion and antagonism.[4] Frameworks of protection are, of course, available in international human rights standards; of paramount importance among these is the safeguarding of freedom of religion or belief: "Everyone has the right to freedom of thought, conscience and religion; this right includes freedom to change his religion or belief, and freedom, either alone or in community with others, and in public or private, to manifest his religion or belief, in worship, teaching, practice and observance."[5] Yet while standards such as these may be necessary in laying down basic rights to protection, they are not sufficient in ensuring those rights; as the shameful tragedy of Bosnian Muslims massacred at Srebrenica demonstrates only too starkly, protection depends on the will of the powerful in any given context to safeguard the rights of the vulnerable. Both Christian and Islamic traditions speak compellingly of the need to protect others. In the latter tradition, the concept of *dhimma* has in its historically institutionalized reality been criticized by many for effectively restricting minorities to a subordinate position. Conversely, Mustafa Ceric, interpreting *dhimma* as the commitment of Muslims to protect the fundamental dignities and entitlements of their non-Muslim neighbors, has lamented that there was no Christian understanding of the same kind available to preserve the Muslims of Srebrenica from genocide.[6] In fact, though not expressed in juridical terms, the injunction to safeguard the vulnerable is a central gospel imperative that Christians in positions of power and influence can and should see as applying to Muslims and to other religious minorities.

Finally, the horizon against which Christians and Muslims can most effectively work together for the common good is that of mutual recognition of each other as peoples engaged not in a merely human project but rather turned together to face toward God. Christian and Islamic understandings of God indeed differ sharply and perhaps irreducibly, but it is still our acknowledgment of one another as people who bear within themselves the transforming burden of the divine Word that is the surest ground on which to build trust, friendship, and cooperation.[7] Nowhere is this openness to God more evident than in contexts of great pain such as Bosnia: "Places and people which have suffered much can become places and people particularly open to the gracious presence of the Spirit."[8] Sarajevo is such a place, and Christians and Muslims are such people.

Notes

1. Couplet written on the foundation stone of the Old Bridge. Mišo Marić, "Once upon a Bridge," in *Stari Most u Mostaru—The Old Bridge in Mostar,* ed. Alija Cigić and Ante Mišković (Mostar: Institut za strojarstvo Sveučilišta u Mostaru, 2004). Extract posted on http://most.ba/ob/content.aspx (accessed June 5, 2008).
2. The Nobel Prize–winning poet Ivo Andrić captured the resonance of the bridge as a symbol of the common good when he wrote: "Bridges are more important than houses and more sacred than temples, because everyone uses them and they belong to everyone." Quoted in *Stari Most u Mostaru,* ed. Cigić and Mišković.
3. *Nostra Aetate,* cap. 3.
4. A practical illustration of what this might mean in the British context can be seen in the guidelines issued by the Inter Faith Network for the UK, *Looking after One Another: The Safety and Security of our Faith Communities,* www.interfaith.org.uk (accessed June 5, 2008).
5. European Convention of Human Rights, Art. 9.1.
6. Mustafa Ceric, "Remembering the Past, Thinking the Present, Dreaming the Future," in *The Road Ahead: A Christian-Muslim Dialogue,* ed. Michael Ipgrave (London: Church House, 2002), 5–12, and cf. 46.
7. For a discussion of this theme in relation to the prophetic traditions of Christianity and Islam, see Michael Ipgrave, *Bearing the Word* (London: Church House, 2005), 124–40.
8. Archbishop Rowan Williams, speech at the closing ceremony of the Fourth Building Bridges seminar, National Theatre, Sarajevo, May 18, 2005.

Index

'Abduh, 165
Abraham, 146–49
Achebe, Chinua, 87
adversarial approach to concept of the
    common good, 85–88
aesthetic perspective, 15–16
al-'Afghānī, 165
Africa
    common good in. *See* West Africa,
        different models of the common
        good in
    "Five Talents" Initiative, 137
Al Qaeda, 170n42
Albigensians, 126n6
Algeria, shurocracy in, 78
Alibasic, Ahmet, x
America. *See* United States
Ammah, Rabiatu, 120
Andrić, Ivo, 178n2
Anglicanism
    British citizenship and, 51, 55
    church-state relations and, 4, 30–32
    English ethnicity, identification with,
        50
    "Five Talents" Initiative, 137
apocalyptic, 150–51
Aristotelianism, 11, 82
Armenia, 30, 32
Arnaud (papal legate), 126n6
asceticism *(zuhd)*, 142–46, 168n18
al-Ash'arī, 161, 167
Ashdown, Paddy, Lord, x, 2n2

Athanasius, 52n63
atheism, 18, 51, 95, 140
Augustine of Hippo, 28, 81, 85, 149
āya (sign) and ayatology, 130, 161–67
Azumah, John, 71, 115

Badawi, Abdullah, 103–4, 113
Badawi, Zaki, 4, 49
Balkan tradition of civic and religious
    identity, 44–46
al-Bāqillānī, 167
Bektović, Safet, 148
belief in God, mutual, recognition of,
    177
believers and citizens. *See* civic sphere,
    believers and citizens in
Berger, Peter, 86
Berry, Wendell, 158, 160
Bible
    Abraham, divergent understandings
        of, 146–49
    church-state relations in, 27–29, 118
    environment in prophetic books of
        Hebrew scripture, 130, 153–60
    Ishmael, significance for Muslims of,
        148–52
    poverty and, 134–37, 152, 171n49
    prosperity gospel, 151
    Serbian Orthodox views of civic and
        faith identity, 41–43, 47
Bin-Laden, Osama, 150, 151, 170n42

blasphemy, English common-law provision against, 52, 57
Bosnia-Herzegovina
    bridge-building between Christians and Muslims in context of, 175–77
    Building Bridges seminar (Sarajevo, 2005), ix–x, 1–2
    Catholics in, identity of, 4, 35–39
    the common good
        Bosnian Muslim views of, 70, 93–96
        personalist approach shared by Muslims and Orthodox Christians, 70, 97–101
    environmental degradation in, 156
    formation of, 35–36
    Kaimije, Ḥasan, 141–42
    Old Bridge, Mostar, 175, 178n1–2
    public holidays in, 36
    Serbian Orthodox views of civic and faith identity, 4, 41–47
Breiner, Bert F., 120–21, 122
bribery, 98–99, 100–101
bridge-building between Islam and Christianity, 1–2, 175–77
    in civic sphere. *See* civic sphere, believers and citizens in
    on common good. *See* the common good, under C
    mutual belief in God, recognition of, 177
    past, purification of memory with regard to, 176
    protection of other faiths, commitment to, 176–77
    symbols of the common good, bridges as, 175, 178n2
    on world issues, 2, 129–31. *See also* environment; poverty

Britain, faith and national identity in, 4–5, 49–58
    blasphemy, common-law provision against, 52, 57
    Catholicism in Britain, 51–52
    Christian attitudes regarding, 55–58
    Church of England. *See* Anglicanism
    concept of citizenship in Britain, development of, 49–51
    incitement to religious hatred, legislation on, 56–58
    Islam
        British citizenship and, 52–55
        critiques and fears of, 18, 52, 55
    multiethnicity, 50, 66n75
    religion and citizenship, 50–52
    religious persecution and tolerance
        development of religious freedom and plurality, 51, 66n76
        new legislation on incitement to religious hatred, 56–58
        political versus theological opposition to non-Anglicans, 51–52
Brown, Richard, x
Buddhism, 106
Building Bridges seminar (Sarajevo, 2005), ix–x, 1–2
Bulgaria, 97, 98, 100
al-Būṣīrī, 143–44
Byzantine empire, 29–30, 97, 99

Cabasilas, Nicolas, 42
Caird, G. B., 155
capital punishment, 84
Cartesian sense of identity, 62n44
Catechism of the Catholic Church, 38
Catholicism
    Bosnia-Herzegovina, identity of Catholics in, 4, 35–39

in Britain, 51–52
Church of England, Catholic revival
    in, 31
Second Vatican Council on Christian
    and Muslim relations, 176
theology of the common good in, 70,
    81–91
    adversarial approach to, 85–88
    individual human rights and,
        84–85
    resolving tension between religious
        traditionalism and secular
        pluralism, 87–91
    traditional understanding of, 81–83
    vagueness of concept, problem of,
        82, 83–84
Ceric, Mustafa (Rais al-Ulama), ix, 1,
    176
cesaropapism, 45
Childs, Brevard, 172n62
Ex. p. Choudhury, 66n78, 67n88
Christianity
    Britain Christian attitudes towards
        faith and national identity, 55–58
    Catholicism. *See* Catholicism
    Church of England. *See* Anglicanism
    church-state relations in, 4, 27–34
    the common good and
        adversarial approach, 85–88
        in Catholic theology. *See* Catholic
            theology of the common good
        in Malaysia, 103, 105–6, 111. *See also*
            Malaysia, government and reli-
            gion in
        personalist approach, 70, 97–101
        in West Africa. *See* West Africa,
            different models of the common
            good in

in developing world, 151–52
diversity, intra-Christian, 51
environment in prophetic books of
    Hebrew scripture, 130, 153–60
Islam, bridge-building with. *See*
    bridge-building between Islam and
    Christianity
Jesus, Islamic association of *zuhd*
    (asceticism) with, 146
liberation theologies, 32, 150, 152
Orthodox churches
    Anglican Non-Jurors and, 31
    personalist approach of, 70, 97–101
    Serbian Orthodox views of civic
        and faith identity, 4, 41–47
poverty and, 134–40, 151–52
Reformation, 30, 51, 118
as religion, 52n63
Second Vatican Council on Christian
    and Muslim relations, 176
West African Muslim view of secular
    state as Christian, 117–18
church and state. *See* civic sphere,
    believers and citizens in
Church of England. *See* Anglicanism
Ciric, Vladimir, 70, 97
citizenship. *See* civic sphere, believers
    and citizens in
civic sphere, believers and citizens in, 2,
    3–5
    Bible, church-state relations in,
        27–29, 118
    in Britain. *See* Britain, faith and
        national identity in
    Catholics in Bosnia-Herzegovina,
        identity of, 4, 35–39
    church-state relations in Christianity,
        4, 27–34

civic sphere (*continued*)
democracy. *See* democracy
Malaysian granting of citizenship to
non-Malays and non-Muslims,
107–8
public versus private identity. *See*
public and private identity in
secular liberal democracies
separation of church and state, 89,
118, 139
Serbian Orthodox views on, 4, 41–47
civilizational Islam *(Islām Hadhāri),*
103–5, 113
climate change, 157
colonial legacy
scientistic theology in Islam, 165, 167
in West Africa, 116–19
the common good, ix–x, 1–2, 69–71
adversarial approach to, 85–88
in Bosnia-Herzegovina
Muslim views on governance and
justice, 70, 93–96
personalist approach shared by
Muslims and Orthodox Christians, 70, 97–101
bridges as symbols of, 175, 178n2
Christian view of. *See under*
Christianity
democracy. *See* democracy
Islamic views of. *See* Islamic views of
the common good
in Malaysia. *See* Malaysia, government and religion in
personalist approach to, 70, 97–101
in West Africa. *See* West Africa,
different models of the common
good in
commonsense perspective, 15–16

compassion in Islam (*rahma* and rahma-
tology), 130, 161–67
Coptic Christians, 30, 97
Corpus Christianum, 29–30
corruption, 98–99, 100–101, 115
Cote D'Ivoire, 116
Cyrus the Persian, 27

dār al-islām, dār a-lharb, and *dār al-sulh*
or *dār al-ahd,* 54, 67n84
Dasgupta, Partha, 138
Davis, Ellen, 129, 130, 153
Dayton Agreements, 35–36
Declaration of Independence, U.S., 32
democracy
American concepts of freedom,
149–50
Islamic views on, 78–79, 94
in Bosnia, 94
in West Africa, 117–20
Democratic Action Party (SDA) in
Bosnia-Herzegovina, 95–96
dhimma, 79, 121, 176
dialogical formation of identity, 10–11
Dignitatis humanae, 90
Diognetus, Epistle to, 33–34
Domitian (Roman emperor), 28, 29
Dwight, Timothy, 171n49

Eastern culture, personalism in, 70,
97–101
Ebionites, 152
ecology. *See* environment
economic issues. *See* entries at poverty
end times, 150–51
engineering attitude in Islam, 173n77
environment
in Hebrew scriptures, 130, 153–60

Islamic ayatology and rahmatology,
    130, 161–67
  poverty of, 138
  thingliness, problem of, 163, 164, 165,
    173n77
eschatology, 150–51
Ethiopia, 30, 32
ethnic issues in Malaysia, 103, 107–8,
    110, 113
evangelism and British religious hatred
    legislation, 57–58
extractive model of Islamic view of the
    common good, 79

al-Faruqi, Isma'il, 117–18
feminism, 9, 18
Figgis, John Neville, 31–32
"Five Talents" Initiative, 137
former Yugoslavia, breakup of, 35, 37,
    93, 98
France, headscarf *(foulard)* case in, 13–14
freedom, American concepts of, 149–50
freedom of religion. *See* religious perse-
    cution and tolerance

Gaudium et spes, 81
Geertz, Clifford, 14–15
Ghana, 115, 116, 120, 121
al-Ghazālī, 12, 20, 145, 161, 164
global issues, 2, 129–31. *See also* environ-
    ment; poverty
global warming, 157
God, recognition of mutual belief in,
    177
Gold Coast, 116
Golden Rule, 106
Gordon Riots (1780), 52
governance and justice. *See* the common
    good

Grameen banks, 137
Graves, Robert, 21, 60n17
Gray, John, 151, 170n42
Great Britain. *See* Britain, faith and
    national identity in
Greek Orthodox. *See* Orthodox Chris-
    tian churches
Gregory Palamas, 61n42

Hagar, 148–49
hate speech, 56–58, 65n70
headscarf *(foulard)* case in France, 13–14
Hebrew Scriptures. *See* Bible
Heschel, Abraham Joshua, 172n58
Hinduism, 106
Ḥizb-ut-Tahrir, 78
holidays, public
    in Bosnia-Herzegovina, 36
    in Malaysia, 109
Hollenbach, David, 38–39
Hudud bill, Malaysia, 112–13
Hulaghu, 94
human rights
    common good, problem of, 84–85
    identity as right, 43, 63n58
    Shari'a, Christian perspective on, 121
Hume, David, 59n8, 83
Husserl, Edmund, 162
Hussites, 30

ibn al-'Arabī, 165, 167
identity. *See* civic sphere, believers and
    citizens in
"imageless act" in Rilke, 7, 23, 25–26
India, Christianity in, 30
Indonesia, 171n50
Institute of Islamic Understanding
    Malaysia, 107

International Islamic University
  Malaysia, 107
Ipgrave, Michael, 4, 49, 175
Iranian revolution, 97–98
Ireland, suppression of bishoprics in, 31
Isaac, 146, 149, 151, 170n43
Isaiah, 158–60
al-Iskandarī, ʿAṭāʾ Allāh, 162–63
Islam
  Abraham, divergent understandings
    of, 146–49
  Britain, faith and national identity in
    citizenship, concepts of, 52–55
    critiques and fears regarding Islam,
      18, 52, 55
  Christianity, bridge-building with.
    See bridge-building between Islam
    and Christianity
  on the common good. *See* Islamic
    views of the common good
  dhimma, concept of, 79, 121, 176
  engineering attitude in, 173n77
  environment and, 130, 161–67
  Ishmael, significance of, 148–52
  Jesus, association of *zuhd* (asceticism)
    with, 146
  millet system, 29
  poverty and, 136, 138–40. *See also*
    option for the poor in Islam
  public and private identity in secular
    liberal democracies
    critiques of modern secular world
      by, 21–26
    modern secular critiques of, 17–21
    religious and secular perspectives,
      continuities of, 14–17
  ritual acts, importance of, 21–22
  scientistic theology in, 165, 167

Second Vatican Council on Christian
  and Muslim relations, 176
Islām Hadhārī (civilizational Islam),
  103–5, 113
Islam in Africa Organization, 118–19
Islamic law. *See* Shariʿa
Islamic Party of Malaysia (*Parti Islam
  Semalaysia,* PAS), 112–13
Islamic views of the common good, 69,
  73–79
  adversarial approach, 85–88
  Bosnian Muslims, 70, 93–96
  common agreements and disagree-
    ments regarding, 73–75
  extractive model of, 79
  general theological principles, 75–77
  literalist model of, 77–78
  in Malaysia. *See* Malaysia, govern-
    ment and religion in
  multiple perspectives in Islamic
    world, 73
  personalist approach, 70, 97–101
  reformist model of, 78–79
  Shariʿa. *See* Shariʿa
  in West Africa. *See* West Africa,
    different models of the common
    good in
Izetbegovic, Alija, 94

Jacobites, 30
James II (king of England), 31
Japan, banning of Exodus in, 171n49
Jeremiah, 154–57, 160
Jesus, Islamic association of *zuhd* (asceti-
  cism) with, 146
Jews and Judaism
  Abraham, divergent understandings
    of, 146–49

church-state relations, 27–28
civic sphere, believers and citizens in, 27–28, 35, 47, 51, 67n87
environment in prophetic books of Hebrew scripture, 130, 153–60
Isaac, triumph of, 146, 149, 151, 170n43
under Islam, 120
poverty and, 130, 134, 136
private and public identity for, 22
Zionism, 119, 152
John Paul II (pope), 37–38, 81, 150
justice
    governance and justice. See the common good
    as political and private virtue, 12–14
    Shari'a. See Shari'a
al-Juwaynī, 164

Ka'ba, 146
Kaimije, Ḥasan, 141–42, 146
Kamali, Mohammad Hashim, 70–71, 103
Kant, Immanuel, 165
Karcic, Fikret, 70, 93, 94–95
Keats, John, 16
Keble, John, 31
Kenya, 115, 121
Khomeini (Ayatollah), 98
King, Martin Luther, Jr., 89
Konràd, Györgu, 65n70
kufr (infidelity), 118, 165–66

Langan, John, 66n77, 70, 81
last days, 150–51
Latic, Dzemaludin, 95–96
Lawrence, T. E., 98
Leibniz, Gottfried Wilhelm, 162
Leo XIII (pope), 81

Levinas, Emmanuel, 62–63n50, 146–48
Lewis, Bernard, 149
liberation theologies, 32, 150, 152
Liberia, 116
Libya, 162
literalist model of Islamic view of the common good, 77–78
liturgical identity of Orthodox Christians, 41–47
Lochhead, David, 68n91
Lollards, 30
Lubardic, Bogdan, 4, 41
Lyussy, Sidi Lahsen, 142

MacIntyre, Alasdair, 9, 12–13
Mahathir, Dr., 108, 110
Malawi, 133
Malay Chinese Association (MCA), 107
Malaysia, government and religion in, 70–71, 101–13
    Constitutional provisions, 106–10
    daily life, 109–10
    economic conditions and, 110–11, 113
    ethnicity, 103, 107–8, 110, 113
    Islām Hadhāri (civilizational Islam), concept of, 103–5, 113
    public holidays, 109
    public life, non-Muslim participation in, 110–12
    religious pluralism and mutual tolerance, 103, 105–6
    Shari'a, 112–13
Malaysian Consultative Council of Buddhism, Christianity, Hinduism and Sikhism (MCCBCHS), 108, 109
Malaysian Interfaith Network, 106
Malik, Maleiha, 3, 4, 7

al-Mālikī, Shaykh Muḥammad 'Alawī, 143, 144, 165

Mandla v. Dowell Lee, 67n87

Manicheans, 168n18

Maritain, Jacques, 84

Marshall, David, x

Marxism, 9, 86, 93

MASPOK, 98

al-Māturīdī, 161, 167

Mawdūdī, 78

Maximus the Confessor, 63n57

Mazrui, Ali, 117

MCA (Malay Chinese Association), 107

MCCBCHS (Malaysian Consultative Council of Buddhism, Christianity, Hinduism and Sikhism), 108, 109

memory, purification of, 176

Milan, Edict of, 29

millet system, 29

Milne, Suemas, 18

Milosevic, Slobodan, 100

Moses, 152, 171n49

Mostar, Old Bridge at, 175, 178n1–2

mountaintop removal, 155

Mulla Ṣadra, 164

multiculturalism, 9, 13, 19, 120

Muslims. *See* Islam

mutual belief in God, recognition of, 177

Myanmar, 133

an-Na'im, Abdullahi Ahmed, 123

National Development Policy (NDP), Malaysia, 110–11

national holidays
  in Bosnia-Herzegovina, 36
  in Malaysia, 109

nationalism, 97–98, 100, 115–16

Nayed, Aref Ali, xi, 60n14, 129, 130, 161

Nazir-Ali, Michael, 4, 27, 61n31

NDP (National Development Policy), Malaysia, 110–11

NEP (New Economic Policy), Malaysia, 110

Nero (Roman emperor), 28

Nestorians, 97

New Economic Policy (NEP), Malaysia, 110

Newbigin, Lesslie, 29

Nicholls, David, 31, 32

Nietzschean sense of identity, 62n44

Nigeria
  Christian perspective in, 122
  colonial legacy in, 116, 121
  development of current political situation in, 116–17
  Ibos, Christianization of, 87
  multifaith culture in, 121
  Muslim desire for Shari'a in, 117–20, 123
  nation-state as problematic concept in, 115

Nikolaj, Metropolitan of Dabar-Bosnia, ix, 1

nomocanonical legal systems, 97, 99, 100

Non-Jurors, 31

Nostra Aetate, 176, 178n3

Oakeshott, Michael, 8

oikoumene, 2, 129–31. *See also* environment; poverty

Old Bridge, Mostar, 175, 178n1–2

ontological sense of identity, 41, 61–62n42–43

option for the poor in Islam, 130, 141–52
  Abraham, divergent understandings
    of, 146–49
  anger of Prophet at poverty of others,
    144–46
  Christian parallels, 151–52
  Ishmael, significance of, 148–52
  Kaimije, Ḥasan, 141–42
  liberation theologies, 150, 152
  prosperity Qur'ān/gospel, 151
  zuhd (asceticism), 142–46, 168n18
Orsolic, Marko, 94
Orthodox Christian churches
  Non-Jurors and, 31
  personalist approach of, 70, 97–101
  Serbian Orthodox views of civic and
    faith identity, 4, 41–47
Ottoman empire, 29, 70, 97, 99, 120,
  161, 164
Oz, Amos, 170n43

papocesarism, 45
Parti Islam Semalaysia (Islamic Party of
  Malaysia or PAS), 112–13
past, purification of memory with regard
  to, 176
Pax Romana, 28
persecution. See religious persecution
  and tolerance
Persian empire, 29
personalist approach to the common
  good, 70, 97–101
Philippines, 32
poverty, 129–30, 133–52
  Christian understanding of, 134–40,
    151–52
  convergence of Christianity and Islam
    regarding, 152

defining, 133–34
environmental, 138
in Jewish tradition, 130, 134, 136
liberation theologies, 32, 150, 152
Muslim understanding of, 136,
  138–40. See also option for the poor
  in Islam
as religious vocation or virtue, 136–37,
  142–46
spiritual, 133–34, 138, 139
preferential option for the poor. See
  option for the poor in Islam
prophetic books of Hebrew scripture,
  environment in, 130, 153–60
prosperity Qur'ān/gospel, 151
protection of other faiths, commitment
  to, 176–77
public and private identity in secular
  liberal democracies, 3, 7–26
  continuity rather than divide
    between, 8–12
  Islam
    critiques of modern secular world
      by, 21–26
    modern secular critiques of, 17–21
    religious and secular perspectives,
      continuities of, 14–17
  neutral public sphere, problematic/
    attractive aspects of, 8–10
  virtues, civic and religious, 12–14
public holidays
  in Bosnia-Herzegovina, 36
  in Malaysia, 109
Puljic, Vinko Cardinal, ix, 1
Pullman, Philip, 20
purification of memory, 176
Puritans, 30–31
Pusat Islam, 107

Al Qaeda, 170n42
Qur'ān and Sunna
    Abraham and Ismael in, 148–49
    āya, raḥma, and the environment,
        130, 161–67
    on common good, 74–77, 106
    end times in, 150–51
    on living in non-Muslim countries,
        53–54
    poverty and, 143, 152
    prosperity Qur'an, 151
    public and private identity, conti-
        nuity of, 22–23
al-Qurṭubī, 150

racism, 18, 46, 55
al-Rāghib al-Iṣfahānī, 168n18
raḥma (compassion) and rahmatology,
    130, 161–67
Ramadan, Tariq, xi, 69, 70, 73
Rawls, John, 59n7, 83, 86
Raz, Joseph, 9, 10
al-Rāzī, 164
Refah Party, Turkey, 98
Reformation, 30, 51, 118
reformist model of Islamic view of the
    common good, 78–79
religious persecution and tolerance
    adversarial approach to common
        good and, 86
    in Britain
        development of religious freedom
            and plurality, 51, 66n76
        new legislation on incitement to
            religious hatred, 56–58
        political versus theological opposi-
            tion to non-Anglicans, 51–52

commitment to protection of other
    faiths, 176–77
Malaysia. *See* Malaysia, government
    and religion in
millet system, 29
principle of religious freedom and
    tolerance, 89–91
in Roman empire and ancient world,
    29–30
Shari'a, 119–20
Rerum novarum, 81
Ricouer, Paul, 10
Rilke, Rainer Maria, 7, 23–24, 25–26,
    59n1
Roman Catholicism. *See* Catholicism
Roman empire, church-state relations
    in, 27–30
Rosenthal, Franz, 95
Rūmi, 144–45
Russia, 90

Sanneh, Lamin, 125
Sanusi, Lamido, 120
Sarah, 149
Sava Nemanjic, 44–46, 65n68
scientific perspective, 15–16
scientism, 165, 167
Scriptures. *See* Bible; Qur'ān and Sunna
SDA (Democratic Action Party) in
    Bosnia-Herzegovina, 95–96
Second Vatican Council on Christian
    and Muslim relations, 176
secularism
    public versus private identity and. *See*
        public and private identity in
        secular liberal democracies
    separation of church and state, 89,
        118, 139

spiritual poverty and, 133–34, 138, 139

tension between religious traditionalism and, resolving, 87–91

Tutu on the secular state, 123

West African Muslim view of secular
state as Christian, 117–18

separation of church and state, 89, 118,
139

Serbia and Montenegro

proposed national anthem, withdrawal of, 100

religious freedom, law on, 65n69

Serbian culture, personalist approach of,
97–101

Serbian Orthodox views of civic and
faith identity, 4, 41–47

Shari'a

Bosnian Muslim views on, 94–95

disagreements within Islam regarding
understanding of, 75

general theological principles behind,
76, 77

in Malaysia, 112–13

nonexclusivity of, 79

poor, responsibility for, 150

redefining, 69

religious freedom and, 119–20

in West Africa, 71, 116–25

Christian perspective, 120–22

Muslim perspective, 117–20

reconciling positions, 122–25

shukr (gratitude or thanks), 165–66

shurocracy, 78

Sierra Leone, 116

sign in Islam (āya and ayatology), 130,
161–67

Skobtsova, Maria, 42, 63n53

South Africa, 121, 133

Sozomen, 29

Spain, end of Muslim power in, 53

Srebrenica, massacre at, 176

state and church. See civic sphere,
believers and citizens in

strip mining, 155

Sudan, 116–17, 119, 121, 122

Sufism, 106, 141–42, 145, 167

Sulaiman, Ibraheem, 117, 124

Sunna. See Qur'ān and Sunna

svetosavlje, 4, 44–45, 64n65, 65n68

Swaziland, 100

Symeon the New Theologian, 42

Synodikon of Orthodoxy, 44

Tabung Haji, 107

al-Taftazānī, 164

Taylor, Charles, 9, 10

terrorism, 150, 151

thingliness, problem of, 163, 164, 165,
173n77

Thomas Aquinas and Thomism, 12,
61n42, 81, 82, 84

Todorova, Maria, 46

tolerance. See religious persecution and
tolerance

Toleration Act of 1689 (Britain), 66n77

Torres, Camillo, 152

Toynbee, Polly, 18

Tractarians, 31

Turkey, 98

Tutu, Desmond, 123

Uganda, 133

Uḥud, battle of, 126n3

Ulysses, Abraham compared to, 146–47,
148

UMNO (United Malay National
    Organisation), 103, 107
United Kingdom. *See* Britain, faith and
    national identity in
United Malay National Organisation
    (UMNO), 103, 107
United States
    church-state relations in, 32
    freedom, concepts of, 149–50
    prosperity gospel in, 151
    strip mining in, 155

Vatican II on Christian and Muslim
    relations, 176
virtue, public and private, 12–14
Vitousek, Peter, 153

Wāhhābism, 152, 171n50
Waldensians, 30
waqf system, 150
Washington, George, 171n49
Weil, Simone, 147, 169n26
West Africa, different models of the
    common good in, 71, 115–25
    Christian perspective, 120–22
    colonial legacy, 116–19
    development of current political situ-
        ation, 116–17
    mistrust, legacy of, 122

multifaith culture, 115–16, 121
Muslim perspective, 117–20
nation-state as problematic concept,
    115–16
reconciling, 122–25
Westermann, C., 149, 152
Whitehouse v. Lemon, 67n86
William and Mary (king and queen of
    England), 31
Williams, Rowan (archbishop of
    Canterbury), ix, 1, 31–32, 63n53,
    129–30, 133, 178n8
Wink, Walter, 29
Winter, Timothy J., 129, 130, 141
world issues, 2, 129–31. *See also* environ-
    ment; poverty
wujūd, 164

Yadudu, Auwalu Hamisu, 119
Yazdgard, Edicts of, 29
Yugoslavia, breakup of, 35, 37, 93, 98
Yunus, Muhammad, 137

Zealots, 152
Žiča Synod of Serb people (1221), 44,
    64n65
Zionism, 119, 152
Žižek, Slavoj, 46
Zovkic, Mato, 4, 35
zuhd (asceticism), 142–46, 168n18